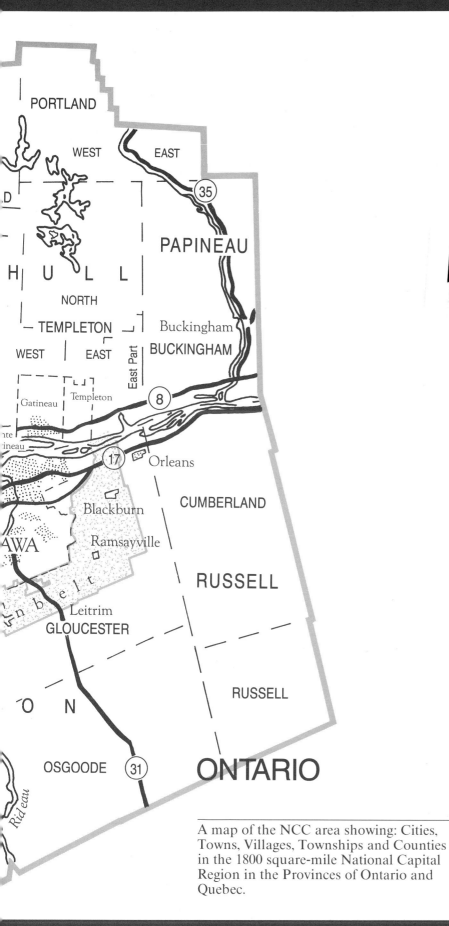

PORTLAND

WEST EAST

35

PAPINEAU

H U L L

NORTH

TEMPLETON

Buckingham

WEST EAST

BUCKINGHAM

East Part

Gatineau Templeton

8

ineau

17 Orleans

CUMBERLAND

Blackburn

Ramsayville

AWA

RUSSELL

n b e l t

Leitrim

GLOUCESTER

RUSSELL

O N

OSGOODE 31

ONTARIO

Rideau

A map of the NCC area showing: Cities, Towns, Villages, Townships and Counties in the 1800 square-mile National Capital Region in the Provinces of Ontario and Quebec.

HARVESTS PAST

Domestic and Agricultural Hand Tools
and Rural Life in the Ottawa Valley
1860 - 1875

To Eric from your
uncle Clyde (Pat) and
on behalf of your aunt
Frances (deceased) with
happy memories and best
wishes.
Pat Patterson
24 August 2004

HARVESTS PAST

Domestic and Agricultural Hand Tools and Rural Life in the Ottawa Valley 1860 - 1875

Pat and Frances Patterson

THE BOSTON MILLS PRESS

Published with the assistance of the Ontario Heritage
Foundation, Ontario Ministry of Culture and Communications.
The research for and development of this work was undertaken
at the initiative of and with financial support from the National
Capital Commission, Canada.

Canadian Cataloguing in Publication Data

Patterson, Clyde R. (Pat) 1918–
    Harvests past

Bibliography: p.
ISBN 1-55046-020-X

1. Implements, utensils, etc. – National Capital
Region (Ont. and Quebec) – History. 2. Agricultural
implements – National Capital Region (Ont. and
Quebec) – History. 3. Tools – National Capital
Region (Ont. and Quebec) – History. 4. Frontier
and pioneer life – National Capital Region (Ont.
and Quebec).   I. Patterson, Frances, 1918–
II. Title.

FC2789.P38 1989   680'.9713'84   C89-094361-3
F1054.09P38 1989

Published by:
THE BOSTON MILLS PRESS
132 Main Street
Erin, Ontario N0B 1T0
(519) 833-2407
FAX (519) 833-2195

American Association
for State and Local History
Award of Merit

Winners of the
Heritage Canada
Communications Award

Design by John Denison
Cover design by Gill Stead
Edited by Paul Litt, Toronto
Typeset by Speed River Graphics
Printed by Ampersand, Guelph

The publisher wishes to acknowledge the financial
assistance and encouragement of The Canada Council,
the Ontario Arts Council and the Office of the
Secretary of State.

CONTENTS

This book is for Dave McIntosh, formerly Adviser,
Communications, National Capital Commission,
himself an author and a long-time tool collector,
who felt that this book should be written,
and felt that we could write it.

ACKNOWLEDGEMENTS

WHEN we look back on the years that we spent gathering information in order to write this book, we find ourselves faced with the difficult task of thanking all who helped us with their knowledge and advice. There were also those who graciously lent items from their own collections for our illustrations. They included friends and neighbours who share our interest in the Ottawa Valley's past, and the acquaintances we made at barn sales, auctions, heritage fairs, in local museums and antique shops or in other collectors' homes.

In particular we wish to express our gratitude for the assistance given by Mr. T.A. Brown, Curator of Agricultural Technology at the National Museum of Science and Technology, who lent an unfailing ear to our questions, sought answers for us, and read and commented upon our text. His efforts were shared by Ms. Minda Bojin, then Museum Librarian, who provided us with a place to work and with historical matter for our research. We appreciated the continuing interest and welcome shown by Doug Walthausen and his staff at the Log Farm of the National Capital Commission. Ms. Judy Tomlyn of the History Division of the then National Museum of Man made many arrangements for us to see people and artifacts. Ms. Jane Foster, the Director of the Lennox and Addington County Museum at Napanee, spent hours setting up items from the museum collections for our photographs. Mr. H. Pietersma, Manager of Agricultural Programming at Upper Canada Village, was generous with his time and advice. Our friends of the Merrickville and District Historical Society, particularly Max and Virginia Martyn, both past presidents of the society, as well as the Parks Canada staff, were interested and supportive throughout the project.

We are grateful for the help of our granddaughter, Tracy Bright. Since early childhood she has shared our interest in the past and is most knowledgeable about hand tools and their history.

We are most grateful for the continued interest in this book demonstrated by Mrs. Jean Pigott, the Chairman of the National Capital Commission. Mrs. Pigott grew up in Ottawa and her love for and pride in the national Capital Region shines through all her activities. Her interest helped to open many doors for us.

We would also like to express our appreciation to Mr. Robert A. Diotte, formerly Manager of Community Relations of the National Capital Commission. Bob was unfailingly co-operative and courteous and never too busy to answer a question or to help solve a problem.

The final work on this manuscript has been done in the restored house which we now occupy in Prince Edward County. We have been fortunate in finding an interested expert and amiable friend in Tom Kuglin, curator of Macaulay Heritage Park in Picton.

During the course of our research we visited, among others, the:

Allan MacPherson House, Napanee, Ontario
Archives of Ontario, Toronto, Ontario
Bellevue Historical Park House, Kingston, Ontario
Bellrock Mill Museum, Bellrock, Ontario
Black Creek Pioneer Village, Downsview, Ontario
Bowmanville Museum, Bowmanville, Ontario
Bytown Museum, Ottawa, Ontario
Cumberland Museum, Cumberland, Ontario
Farm Museums, Cooperstown, New York
Fort Wellington National Historic Park, Prescott, Ontario
Gananoque Museum, Gananoque, Ontario
Grenville County Historical Society Museum, Prescott, Ontario
Halton Regional Museum, Milton, Ontario
Highland Museum, Kingussie, Scotland
Long Island Mill, Manotick, Ontario
MacLachlen Woodworking Museum, Kingston, Ontario
National Archives Canada, Ottawa, Ontario
Ontario Agricultural Museum, Milton, Ontario
Ross Farm Museum, New Ross, Nova Scotia
Shelburne Museum, Shelburne, Vermont
Sherbrooke Village, Sherbrooke, Nova Scotia
Strawbery Banke, Portsmouth, New Hampshire
Williamstown Loyalist and Nor'western Museum, Williamstown, Ontario.

PREFACE

THE celebration of Canada's 100th birthday in 1967 brought a renewed pride in our forebears and a surge of interest in our country's past. What were Canadians like a century ago? How did they live and work? Questions such as these have stimulated a growing demand for source books illustrating the appearance, use and operation of the hand tools, implements and utensils that are being assembled in public and private collections as evidence of earlier stages in rural life in Canada.

This book sets out to illustrate who used what hand tools and for what purpose during an important developmental period in the National Capital portion of the Ottawa Valley. In writing about the tools used during a specific time, one is always constrained by the fact that although it is easy to tell what was available, it is difficult to be sure how much things were actually used. People then were probably much as they are today. There were undoubtedly those who took advantage of every new idea and others who were convinced that what had been good enough for their fathers would suit them just fine. There were as yet no mail order catalogues in the homes, so new ideas in tools and domestic utensils probably came from advertisements in periodicals and newspapers, from the stock of a travelling pedlar, from hardware catalogues supplied to merchants or by word of mouth. So-called improvements might well be regarded with suspicion. For example, some women apparently had difficulty coping with the cook stove at first, and missed open hearth cooking despite all its tribulations and hazards.

It is important to remember that, for many, cash was hard to come by. When it was available, expenses such as taxes and payments on land had to be met first. In any one period of time neighbouring families might be a world apart in their way of life, depending upon when they had arrived in the Ottawa Valley, what kind of land they were cultivating and whether they had some supplementary source of income such as a military pension.

Almost from the beginning of large-scale settlement, the population of the National Capital area consisted mostly of English, Irish and Scottish settlers from Britain, French-speaking Canadians who came from down the St. Lawrence River to work on the Rideau Canal and in the lumber camps, plus newcomers from the United States. One of the reasons for the compromise choice of Ottawa as the nation's capital city at a later date was that it had a population which represented, in sizable numbers, both founding peoples. The various settlers brought with them their own approach to daily life, whether they had learned it in Trois Rivières or in Glasgow. What makes the people of the Valley so unique is the blending of the Irish, Scots, English and French with the original inhabitants, the Algonquins. Add a touch of Yankee ingenuity and you find an extraordinary inheritance.

In researching rural life on both sides of the Ottawa River, one is impressed, not with the differences in home and farming practices and their tools and implements, but rather with the similarities that existed. Unless the tool was made by an individual farmer or crafstman such as a blacksmith, there was a high degree of similarity among the tools that were brought with, supplied to, or purchased locally by the Ottawa Valley settler. After having collected artifacts from the whole area, our experience has been that the variations are usually related to the requirements and possibilities of the local geography. Thus there are more woods tools and blueberry pickers in one area, more corn planters and cutters in another.

The list of hand tools and equipment discussed is not exhaustive because it would be extraordinary if a farmer maintained a full set of blacksmith equipment or of cabinet maker's tools, when his main purpose in life was farming. We have tried to illustrate the rich breadth of useful, attractive, curious or unique equipment that we know was used over a range of farms and in villages in the Confederation era.

For the authors, the joy of collecting reaches its peak in the discovery of interesting variations of hand tools. In this book we have dealt only with those available for use in home and field by rural families in the Ottawa area between 1860 and 1875. We have visited agricultural museums in continental Europe, the British Isles, the United States and Canada and have never ceased to be impressed by the universal nature of such tools. For example, a bow saw purchased at a flea market in Brussels proved to be almost identical in style to one exhibited in a Roman museum in Cirencester, England.

There is something particularly gratifying about holding in one's hands an object that has been held and used by so many other hands and activated by human energy. In the case of wooden artifacts, the user's hands or feet have sometimes actually left wear marks. Whether the tool has been handed down in one family or the past owner is unknown, it would be an unimaginative collector who did not find pleasure in identifying, caring for and sometimes even using these visible reminders of a heritage of craftsmanship.

With the passing of the years we are naturally and progressively further removed from direct contact with those who can remember someone actually working with these tools. When we first began to haunt Ottawa Valley country auctions over 30 years ago we were quite often approached by elderly gentlemen who had watched us bid on and acquire an old tool. The first question was if we knew what we had bought and if we knew its use. Usually at some point in the ensuing conversation something similar to "I mind my father/mother, grandfather/grandmother using one of those" was said. This seldom happens now, even though many of these tools continued to be used by some well into the twentieth century. Either we now appear to be of an age to know what we are buying, or the generation who remembers their use is no longer spry enough to get around much. Whatever the reason, we miss the opportunity to learn from them and to hear the anecdotes which so often accompanied the explanation.

It is important to remember that there were, as among any group of rural people, those who found the life too hard and left the farms and villages. There were also those who sold their land grants for profit and those who simply drifted off to live elsewhere. The people we write about are those who remained and contributed to the development of their farms and their community. We have included the two main population centres of Ottawa and Hull only insofar as their existence nearby and their histories and development influenced the way of life in the rural areas around them.

Life in the mid-nineteenth century in rural areas like the Ottawa Valley was no bed of roses. A stroll through any country burying ground and a study of the dates on the headstones will prove that, for many, life was comparatively short. Stories handed down in the Valley would seem to tell us that these people not only worked hard and long but that many filled what leisure hours they had with some pretty roistering fun. In other words they were, much like the occupants today, interesting mixtures of saint and sinner.

Picturesque Canada,
1882.

L'ANGE GARDIEN.

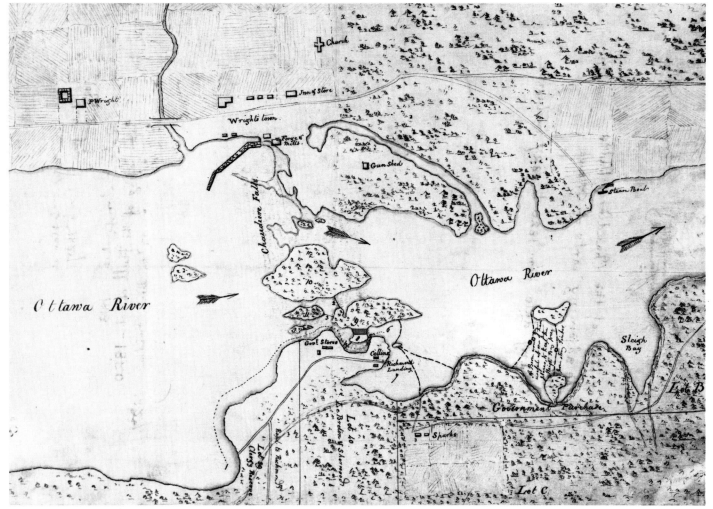

1825 map of the Ottawa River at the Chaudière Falls, showing Wrightstown on the
north shore and Richmond Landing on the south, by Major G.A. Eliot. - PAC NMC-3163

HISTORICAL NOTES

THE Constitutional Act of 1791 divided the former province of Quebec into Upper and Lower Canada. The Act of Union of 1840 re-united these units into one Province of Canada, in which the old colonies were known as Canada West and Canada East. It was not until Confederation in 1867 that the provinces were formally named Ontario and Quebec. Since all these names were in use during the time span of this book, and since people tended to use the old names for a time after the new ones were given, we have taken the historical liberty of using the names "Ontario" and "Quebec" throughout the text.

Philemon Wright's village is also referred to by several names, but we have used the name of "Wrightstown" throughout. Another confusion that arises in this respect is the tendency of the time to shorten the word "Township" to "Town". Wright, in some of his own account books, identifies himself as being of the "Town of Hull." It was actually many years after his death that the village he founded took the name of the whole Township.

It is impossible to write of the history of the artifacts of the National Capital Region without mentioning the sad record of the fires that have plagued the area. Because of the piles of lumber drying everywhere in Ottawa and Hull at the peak of the lumbering days, because so many houses were built of wood, because of the wasteful way of lumbering which left piles of tinder-like waste behind, because of the use of open flames for light and heat, and because of the shortage of water to fight fires once they began, the history of the region is marked by stories of destruction by fire. Even a single home destroyed by flames meant the loss of a piece of history, but the fires that raged through large areas meant not only human misery, but the loss of historic structures and their contents, as well as records and documents. No other city in Canada has suffered such fire damage as has been inflicted on the city of Hull. Twice its city hall has been burned, with the loss of irreplaceable records each time. Almost every one of the original buildings of Philemon Wright has been lost to us by fire or demolition. For this reason the occupants of the National Capital Region, and indeed all Canadians, would appear to have the responsibility of taking special heed that what is left be preserved for generations to come.

"A view of the Mill and Tavern of Philemon Wright at the Chaudière Falls on the
Ottawa River, Lower Canada." H.Y. DuVernet, 1823. - PAC C608

CHAPTER 1
PART I — BEGINNINGS

THIS book is about a group of people and how they lived and worked, and the tools and implements they used in their homes and on their farms. The people are those who lived in the area now known as the National Capital Region, and the time is the period from 1860 to 1875. It will be easier to understand their mode of life if we go back in time far enough to find out where they came from, and what brought them to live in the valley of the Ottawa River.

The National Capital Region consists of an area of roughly 470,000 hectares (1800 square miles), bisected by the Ottawa River, including most of Carleton County and small parts of Russell and Lanark Counties in Ontario, and parts of the Counties of Pontiac, Papineau, Gatineau and Hull in Quebec.

The river now known as the Ottawa had been used by the native people for transport from time immemorial. In the days of New France it became an important route for the transport of furs. All travellers on the river had to portage around the falls situated between what is now Ottawa to the south and Hull to the north. The Algonquins had given the rapids the name of "Asticou" or "Kettle" because of its furiously boiling waters, and when they camped beside it, it was their custom to toss tobacco leaves into the rushing water to mollify the Great Spirit. The month of June, 1988 marked exactly 375 years since Samuel de Champlain used the portage on his way up the river as he searched for a western route to the Orient. He was probably the third European to come this way, but he was the first to record his journey, and in his journals he translated the name of the rapids as "la Chaudière", and that name survives today. The river itself was known to the French as "la Grande Rivière du Nord" and to the English as the "Grand", until it took the name of "l'Outaouais" or "Ottawa" from the name of one of the native tribes who used it to transport their furs.

By the 1780s settlement was proceeding vigorously on the upper St. Lawrence and the Great Lakes from Cataraqui (Kingston) to the area around Niagara, but in the valley of the Ottawa the Algonquins roamed almost undisturbed by settlers. The first white resident seems to have been one Joseph Mondion who established a trading post near Chats Falls in 1786. By 1800 he had apparently gone, leaving the name of Mondion's Point on Lac Deschênes as the sole reminder of his existence.

In March of the year 1800 the remarkable Philomen Wright brought his wife and children and a group of other New Englanders to become the first permanent settlers in the Ottawa Valley. It would be difficult to imagine a man more suited to lead in the establishment of a new community in the wilderness. He came from a prosperous family long settled in Woburn, Massachusetts, and had been successfully involved in both lumbering and farming. He was seeking the two things which were becoming rare in his home region, virgin timber and unoccupied fertile land. After several exploratory visits he found what he was seeking on the north side of the Chaudière Falls, with the added advantage of the falls to run the mills he planned to build. The land he chose had already been surveyed under the English land system, and the Township had been given the name of Hull.

Wright brought with him family groups familiar with frontier living, as well as horses, oxen, agricultural implements, carpenters' tools, mill irons, household effects and provisions. He timed the arrival for the early spring, so he could use the still-frozen river for the last stage of the trip, but spare his people a winter of privation before they began to clear their new land. The first autumn they harvested vegetables and wheat, and by 1804 they had established a sawmill, a hemp mill, grist mills, a distillery and a tannery, as well as shops for a shoemaker, a baker and a tailor. All this had nearly exhausted Wright's capital, and in 1806 he and his son Tiberius were ready to begin what they hoped would be their first money-making project, that of rafting squared logs down the Ottawa River to Quebec City for export to England. Everyone had assured them that it could not be done, but they and their small crew of three accomplished the seemingly impossible. So began the saga of the great squared timber rafts which were to continue to make their way down the river for the next 100 years.

While Wrightstown was beginning to expand and flourish, on the south side of the Ottawa only scattered settlement was taking place. Shortly after the Wright party arrived at the Chaudière, Abijah Dunning and his four sons had settled on land near what is now Cumberland Village. Amable Foubert established a trading post nearby around 1807. That same year a Jehiel Collins built a dock and store at a canoe landing across from Wrightstown. When his clerk Caleb Bellows took over the business shortly after, it became known as Bellows' Landing. In 1811 Ira Honeywell and his family became the first settlers in Nepean Township, and a year later Braddish Billings built a cabin in Gloucester.

Events in Europe were now to shape the future of this scattered group of adventurous settlers among the great timber stands of the Ottawa Valley. Britain and France were at war, and England's navy had an urgent need for tall, clear timber for masts and spars, and for the massive squared logs of oak and pine of which the wooden ships of the day were built. The American Revolution had cut off Britain's access to New England timber, leaving the Baltic countries as the sole source of supply. Then, in 1806, Napoleon issued the Berlin Decree which blockaded British ports against Baltic timber, and Britain turned to Canada to supply her needs. It was sheer coincidence that this was the same year that the first raft made its way down the Ottawa, but it changed the course of history for the occupants of the Valley, and eventually led to the building of a capital city in the virtually uninhabited mixture of swamp and forest across the river from Philemon's village.

After the War of 1812, settlement of Ontario began to assume a different pattern. The British, fearing another American invasion, began to discourage large-scale immigration from the United States, and to encourage settlers to come from Europe, particularly from the British Isles, by offering free land and free passage. Political instability in Europe, unemployment after the end of the Napoleonic Wars, clearances in Scotland, displacement because of the Industrial Revolution and the potato famine in Ireland all added to the pressures for emigration. Ships that had delivered timber and grain to British ports offered cheap rates to passengers rather than return with empty holds. Conditions during the crossing were often appalling, and many did not survive the journey, but still they came, drawn by hunger for land of their own, and the hope of a better life for their children.

A settlement at Richmond, south of Bellow's Landing, was the first group placement in the region. The end of the War of 1812 found many British officers and men stationed in Quebec with no prospect of being needed for active service. The British government felt that a double purpose could be achieved by giving the soldiers varying grants of land according to their rank, thus providing a large number of new settlers, and at the same time, establishing a military presence to discourage any idea of further military aggression from the United States. The site for the future town was selected on the Jock River in Goulbourn Township, and a precise town plan laid out before any settlers arrived.

About 400 soldiers and their families came from Quebec City in the summer of 1818, arriving at Bellows' Landing. It had been decided to name the new town "Richmond" after the newly appointed Governor General of Canada, the Duke of Richmond, and so the name of Bellow's Landing was changed to Richmond's Landing. The women and children spent the rest of the summer in temporary shelters here, while the men hacked a narrow road through the bush for about 25 kilometers (15 miles) to the Jock River, which was then used to transport the settlers about 5 kilometers more (3 miles) to their new town. This road, which is paralleled closely by the Richmond Road of today, was the first road in the Ottawa Valley.

To enable the soldiers and their families to survive in their new life, each had been granted a year's food rations. The head of each family also received one axe, one broadaxe, one mattock, one pickaxe, one spade, one shovel, two scythe stones, two files, one camp kettle, one bed tick, one blanket, twelve panes of glass, one pound (450g) putty and 12 pounds (5.4 kg) nails (in three sizes). In addition, to every five families were allotted a cross-cut saw, a whip saw and a grindstone. The whole settlement was to share two complete sets of carpenters' tools and two sets of blacksmiths' tools. Whatever the soldiers' previous experience had been with such civilian implements, the new settlers managed to establish themselves in homes of some kind by Christmas. It would be a challenge indeed to identify positively one of these original tools, some of which may still rest in old buildings around Richmond. As far as the authors are aware this has not yet been done.

Under the benign supervision of Philemon Wright, his settlement continued to grow. The year after the Richmond Road was built the first road in Hull Township was cut through the bush to Lac Deschênes. This is the Aylmer Road of today, and at the time of its building it provided for the first time a reasonably good portage route around the Chaudière.

While settlements were springing up here and there in the Valley, the site of the future city of Ottawa remained almost uninhabited. Change came suddenly, again brought about by a decision made far away in London, England. The British Admiralty had long been aware of the problems that could arise if British North America should be threatened again from the United States. It would be very difficult to maintain a supply route West because of the vulnerability to American guns of transport through the rapids on the St. Lawrence River between Montreal and Lake Ontario. A canal system to bypass these rapids seemed the only answer, and in 1826, Lieutenant-Colonel John By of the Royal Engineers arrived in Canada with orders to join the Ottawa River to Kingston by way of the Rideau and Cataraqui Rivers. Again the Valley was to gain from the fact that a man of remarkable qualities arrived at a crucial time in its history.

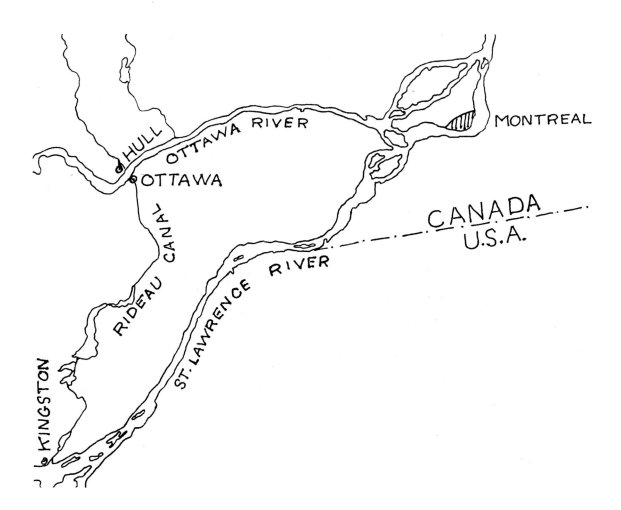

A map of the Canadian-American section of the St. Lawrence River between
Montreal and Lake Ontario. - AUTHOR'S SKETCH

After careful consideration of many sites, By chose the place where the Rideau River joined the Ottawa as the starting point for the canal, and laid out plans for a town across the river from Wrightstown. Master stone masons were brought from the British Isles to supervise the canal stonework, and British military engineers planned and directed the project, but the actual labourers were mostly French-Canadians from Quebec City and Montreal and newly-arrived immigrants from Ireland. Colonel By soon realized that the major population centre and source of supplies was Wrightstown and that the two sides of the river had to be connected by an all-weather link, so his men, with the assistance of Philemon Wright, built the Union suspension bridge, no mean engineering feat in its day.

The Rideau Canal was opened in 1832, and remains an almost incredible achievement, considering the terrain through which it was built, the climate, the inexperienced labourers, the mosquitos and malaria, and the primitive tools available. Financially it never paid its way, and the invasion threat from the south never materialized, but it brought instant growth to the new settlement of Bytown, and eventually was another factor in its choice as the capital city. The soldiers came first, then the labourers, and soon the tradesmen, merchants and professionals to look after their needs. Since all these new residents had to be fed, the neighbouring farmers could sell the spare produce from their farms for cash in the Bytown markets. The soldiers had been promised land grants, so many of them remained in Canada when the canal was finished, adding their skills to those of other immigrants. Some of the stonemasons too, decided to cast their lot in with the settlers, and have left fine stonework throughout the Valley as a memorial to their skill.

On the North side of the Ottawa the growth of Wrightstown slowed as Bytown grew. The paternal type of leadership provided by Philemon Wright did not appeal to all settlers, and many preferred a society not dominated by one family. Philemon Wright died in 1839 but the Wright influence continued through his two surviving sons.

Up and down the Valley, on both sides of the river, scattered settlements grew up as people came, drawn by the growing lumber industry. Some had means and education, and came looking for a challenge or for adventure, but most were of humbler origins, and came to find security and a brighter future. Among the immigrants, labourers and farmers were the most numerous, then followed carpenters, miners, shoemakers, tailors, household servants, blacksmiths and masons. Those who came as steerage passengers could bring little with them; clothes, a few household possessions, a spinning wheel perhaps, or maybe some treasured tools. What they did bring that was to be of far more importance to the Valley and to Canada in the long run, was a heritage of skills and culture from their own lands. They adapted the domestic and agricultural tools of their forebears to a new life in a new world, and these blended with the culture and skills of the native people and the French Canadians, to evolve gradually into a new culture and way of life.

Pakenham village in the 1860s. - AUTHOR'S SKETCH FROM AN EARLY PHOTOGRAPH

CHAPTER 1
PART II — EXPANSION

THE decades following the completion of the Rideau Canal saw the establishment of a pattern of permanent settlement throughout the Ottawa Valley. By 1860 the population of the old Bytown had reached about 14,000. It had been renamed "Ottawa" and had been chosen as the capital city of the United Province of Canada in 1857. Already the Gothic Parliament Buildings were rising on the horizon, and in 1866 the first session of the Provincial Legislature was held in the new structures. The next year it became the capital of the new Dominion.

Across the Ottawa River, Wrightstown was emerging as an industrial centre. It would not become a city and take the name of Hull until 1875. Aylmer, founded by Philemon Wright's nephew Charles Symmes after a falling out with his uncle, was still rivalling Wrightstown in growth, and still was the seat of justice for the Township. On both sides of the river villages and town had grown up, with farms clustered around them. Often the business of supplying the lumber camps determined the pattern of settlement. Owing to the bad roads in the Gatineau Valley, heavily laden supply sleighs could cover only about 21 kilometres (13 miles) a day, so communities such as Chelsea, Wakefield and Low grew up at intervals of about that distance to provide food and shelter for the drivers. Similarly, a horse-drawn cart could travel from Ottawa to South March in one day, and to Arnprior the next. Stopping places grew up in March Township to provide shelter along the route.

If settlers had any choice of location on arrival, they tended to go to areas where they had friends or relatives, or where others who had the same racial origins or spoke the same language lived. This was particularly true of the French-Canadians. In Ontario many settled in the Township of Gloucester, where Cyrville, Embrun and Orleans were founded by francophones. In Quebec the French-speaking settlements were located mostly around Ste-Cecile-de-Masham, Pointe-Gatineau, St.-Pierre-de-Wakefield and Angers (Ange-Gardien). The present day city of Hull, founded by an American, was English-speaking to begin with, but the census of 1870 showed it to be equally English and French.

In 1854 the first cars of the Bytown and Prescott Railway puffed their way into New Edinburgh, heralding the time to come when railroads would replace the waterways as the chief method of transportation of goods in the Valley, eventually ending the colourful era of the squared timber raft. For the 1860s and 70s, however, rivers and canals were still enjoying a heyday, and their waters were full of every type of craft from canoes to steamboats. Roads were impassable for part of each year. In built-up areas, including Ottawa, they were constructed and maintained by statute labour. This meant that every man between 21 and 60 worked a fixed number of days each year, based on his property assessment. Supervisors were called pathmasters. It was a very unsatisfactory system, for inexperienced workers were supervised by their own neighbours. In less built-up areas roads were developed and maintained by private companies which charged tolls. All roads were, by today's standards, very bad, and were to remain so for many years. However, compared to the Indian and animal trails they replaced, they were certainly an improvement.

Newspapers were an early and important part of the development of the Valley. The Ottawa *Citizen* was first published in 1843 as a weekly under the name of the *Packet*. By 1851 it had changed its name, and later became a daily. Weekly papers were published in several of the larger towns. Much can be learned of Valley life by reading the yellowed pages of those which have been preserved. Cash was still scarce and barter was the order of the day. A letter sent to the Carleton Place *Herald* on September 29, 1862, requested that an advertisement about a lost cow be placed in the paper. Someone on the staff of the newspaper has written at the bottom of the letter, "Paid by 1 bag of apples." The Merrickville *Chronicle* of Friday, March 15, 1861, stated that Henry Parker's Tin shop would take old iron, brass, copper, lead, rags and all kinds of farm produce in exchange for goods. The Aylmer *Times* advertised itself as the only newspaper in the Counties of Ottawa and Pontiac. Its subscription rate was $1.50 a year, and it carried advertisements from Montreal, Quebec City and Ottawa. It featured news from Dublin, Ireland, and from London, England, carried by the Atlantic cable and only five days old. From 1861 to 1865 when the American civil war was being fought there was coverage of all major battles. Many stories were carried about the doings of the British royal family and the public appearances of Canadian political figures. To show that some things have not changed, the Aylmer *Times* in its issue of August 12, 1866, reported that the Tuesday before a jeweller's shop in Brantford had been robbed of money and 160 watches.

The villages and towns provided both work and recreation for the farm families nearby. Rural areas were more self-sufficient than they would ever be again. The successful farmer was a jack-of-all-trades and supplied a major portion of his family's needs. There was seldom need to go more than a day's ride on horseback to buy or sell. It was possible to find quite elderly rural residents who had never been to Ottawa or Wrightstown. Never again would neighbours be as important to each other. Many tasks could be speeded up and made more bearable by a neighbourhood "bee". Tales abound of barn-raising, quilting, stumping, corn-husking, logging, paring, plucking, fencing and harvesting bees. At the end of the day of co-operative labour the women would serve a substantial meal, often accompanied by whisky, and there would be dancing until dawn to the music of the famed Ottawa Valley fiddlers. Most people found their marriage partners among their neighbours, probably meeting them at church, at a bee, at another wedding, or even at a wake. Usually a neighbour would assist at the birth of a baby, and a group of neighbours would sit up with the body at the time of death, and walk behind the wagon carrying the body to the grave they had helped to dig.

For a rural family the working day began when the sun rose and did not end until there was no longer light enough to see by, but that did not mean that there was no time for recreation. Cricket was still popular, and regular matches were played between teams from neighbouring towns. The new game of baseball was catching on. Fishing and swimming were among the summer pleasures. Fall fairs were important, not only as social events but also for the upgrading of stock, and as an opportunity for the women to display their household skills. Winter was the best time for exchanging visits and attending meetings, since the farm work was not so pressing, the roads were at their best, and sleighs could speed over the fields and frozen waterways. Curling, skating, snowshoeing, tobogganning and horse racing on ice were all popular recreations. There were many fraternal organizations and societies, and political meetings could occur at any time of year.

The church provided a social focus as well as a spiritual one. After the family, it was probably the most important influence in pioneer life. On many farms only the essential chores were done on Sunday, and only cold meals were served. Families would spend a large part of the day getting to and from church and listening to long sermons. In the lumber shanties Sunday was a day to rest and tidy up, and sometimes hear a sermon from a travelling priest or minister. While horse-drawn streetcars had come to Ottawa by 1870 they were not allowed to run on Sundays.

Excessive drinking seems always to have been part of frontier life. For the settlers the cheap and easily available whisky could provide a temporary escape from hardships that must have appeared overwhelming at times, accompanied as they often were by homesickness for the native country left behind forever. In response to the growing problem, temperance societies were founded, which gradually belied their name by demanding total abstinence. Moderation in drinking apparently was rare; the population became divided between those who drank freely and those who were militantly opposed to anyone taking even a drop. Whisky was sold almost everywhere, some general stores even providing it free to their good customers. Many a country fair ended in a near riot. Any remark could lead to a donnybrook, the most dangerous topics being religion, race, politics and fence lines between neighbours. When a quarrelsome mood prevailed, even a remark about the weather might provoke a general mêlée.

A description of the composition of a typical Valley town as it existed around the time of Confederation will give us an insight into the way the townspeople and those whose farms lay around the town lived their daily lives. Pakenham, founded in 1823, was built beside rapids on the Mississippi River to provide power for its mills. The only sizeable centre for some distance, it was at its peak in the 1860s. The population of around 800 was mostly English, Irish and Scottish. There were at least three doctors and a pharmacist. There was a post office and a library, a school and three churches. In winter the stage ran three times a week to Ottawa. There were numerous merchants and tradesmen, including a fanning-mill maker, dressmakers, a baker, a blacksmith, coopers, carpenters, a harnessmaker, a cabinet maker, tailors, a tinsmith, shoemakers and a wagon and sleigh maker. The general stores carried such merchandise as hardware, groceries, crockery, harness, parasols, gloves, muslins, shawls, bonnets, ribbons, sugar, tobacco, scythes, axes, rakes, gentlemen's boots and hats and ladies morocco and prunella boots and slippers. The stores were often open from 6 a.m. to 10 p.m. The taverns had to be licensed and were subject to inspection. A town hall had been built and was used for meetings. Among the organizations to which one could belong were the Sons of Temperance, the Orange Order and the Vigilance Committee. There was also a notary public and an agent for a Life Insurance Company. The Commercial Hotel was a bustling place, and shops unknown in the 1850s were appearing, such as grocery, butcher, millinery and paint stores.

Log House. – CANADA FARMER, 1864, NATIONAL MUSEUMS OF CANADA

CHAPTER 2
HOME AND FARMYARD

Good husband without it is needful there be
Good housewife within is as needful as he.
Canada Farmer, Toronto
January 15, 1864, Vol. I

BY THE middle of the nineteenth century immigration from Britain to the Ottawa area had passed its peak. The *Canada Farmer* for April 15, 1871, however, still carried an Ontario government advertisement offering free lands to immigrants. Actually, between 1855 and 1879 comparatively few British arrived. Most established Valley farmers prospered with the growth of the lumber industry. Except for the trickle of newcomers the pioneer era was over. It was a stable period — widespread mechanization lay in the future. Many of the substantial homes which lend such charm and variety to the countryside today date from this time.

The evolution of the farm home followed a similar pattern for most settlers. The shanty, built as a shelter for the difficult years, was replaced as soon as possible by a log house containing several rooms, and often a partial cellar. Here the family lived while they cleared their land and acquired stock. The shanty usually became a hen or pig house. During this time the large frame barn was built, often with the help of neighbours, and smaller farm buildings, constructed of whatever material was in greatest supply, were added as needed. When the farmer felt success was assured, the log house was enlarged, or a new house was built, of wood or stone or brick, depending somewhat upon the material most abundant locally. If not incorporated into the new home, the log house became a farm out-building. Families were usually large and extended, so the new houses were often sizeable — two or even three storeys high. The pioneer family had toiled hard and was not averse to demonstrating its success to the neighbours. The new homes often had large rooms and the ceilings were high to accommodate the maze of pipes from the new kitchen and parlour stoves which usually provided the only heat for the upstairs rooms.

The home played such an important role in the life of the day that considerable sacrifices might be made to provide a substantial one. It should be remembered that home was where most people were born, from where most people would be married and where most would die. The Valley farmer had every reason to believe that he and his descendants would live out their lives in the house he built. He had no way of knowing that by the 1870s the great days of wheat growing were already over in Eastern Canada, and that mechanization would develop the Western grainlands. The same pressures for new land and a better life and the same sense of adventure that had brought settlers to Ontario and Quebec would carry many of their descendants to pioneer in the West.

In the more remote areas where the land was poorer, and among new settlers, or

Boot scraper.
- BLOCKHOUSE MUSEUM,
MERRICKVILLE

Wooden bootjack.
- BLOCKHOUSE MUSEUM,
MERRICKVILLE

Cistern pump.
- AUTHORS' COLLECTION

those who had not been able to adapt to the new land, the log houses often remained, and methods of cultivation and domestic life continued to be almost as primitive as in pioneer days.

The kitchen in the new home, as in the old, was the heart of the house, and the family and most visitors used the kitchen entrance. Outside the kitchen was the well, placed to serve both barn and house. The rain barrel stood under the eaves as a source of soft water. The kitchen garden was placed as close as possible, and a path led to the privy. The closest farm buildings were probably the hen house and dairy, since they were usually the responsibility of the women and children. Since farmyards were often muddy or snowy, a metal boot scraper was fastened outside the kitchen door, and inside it a wooden or metal boot jack assisted in the removal of high boots.

In some farm homes rainwater had been diverted to a cistern in the cellar and from there a system of pipes carried it to a cistern pump beside the sink. Used water ran into a pail underneath, or was piped outside into a bed of gravel. Some kitchens had dry sinks made of stone, wood or zinc. They were just what the name implied, having no piped water supply, but they were an improvement over a bucket and basin.

From the 1850s kitchen furniture remained much the same for many years. The cook stove dominated the room just as the hearth had done, and nearby was the woodbox. There was usually an open dish dresser with storage underneath, a bucket bench, a long pine table and wooden benches and chairs, often including a rocker. The flop bench (or settle bed or banc-lit) provided a place for the farmer to snatch forty winks after a hearty meal before going back to the fields, and also a bed for company. Open shelves in kitchen and pantry held supplies in covered containers to protect them against mice and insects. Drawers were few, and most utensils were hung on the walls. Covered boxes held salt and candles, and open wall boxes were used for miscellaneous articles such as string. Nothing that might come in handy was ever thrown away. Some wall boxes held cutting knives and others had been notched to hold spoons. Match holders of many different shapes were usually made of tin or cast iron.

If the house had a cellar, perishables could be stored there. If not, a ventilated root house was excavated on the north side of the house. It had to be dug below frost level, and was entered by means of a ladder or a set of steps. Leading off the kitchen proper was a summer kitchen, usually of unfinished wood, with a large door to provide cross-ventilation. Firewood for immediate consumption was stored at one end or in an attached woodshed. The summer kitchen provided a spot to keep out-of-season articles, and afforded cold storage in winter, as well as a place to cook in summer without heating up the whole house.

The rest of the home varied according to the financial situation of the family and its aspirations. There would certainly be a parlour, heated and used only on special occasions, with the curtains drawn to protect the rugs and furniture. A parlour organ or piano was considered a status symbol. There might also be a second parlour or sitting room and a dining room. There commonly was at least one bedroom downstairs and several upstairs. These would be so cold in winter that they would be used only for sleeping. All these large rooms filled up with large new factory-made furniture and Victorian embellishments as the family could afford

Kitchen scene at the Log Farm Museum, Nepean.
- T. ATKINSON, NATIONAL CAPITAL COMMISSION

them. The real gathering place of the family still remained the kitchen, always the warmest part of the house in winter, and always brimming with activity.

Every farm family was as self-sufficient as possible. They met most of their own needs, and bartered for things they themselves did not grow or make. The cash they earned by the sale of extra products to the lumber camps and to town and city residents would be devoted to such necessities as the payment of taxes, upgrading of stock and home or the purchase of more land or equipment. No farm could succeed without co-operation between adults and all children old enough to help. While the men and older boys had as their responsibility the fields and woods and stables, and the women and younger children the home and garden and dairy, the men were called upon from time to time to help out with heavier household tasks such as moving stoves to and from the summer kitchen, and the women helped when needed in the fields. So difficult was it to operate a farm without a partner, that weddings of convenience were common. There are tales of women left widowed who managed to survive with the help of children until the older boys reached maturity, but it was a herculean task.

Among the unsung heroines of the Valley past are the wives of the shanty farmers. These were the men who went into the woods in the late fall to work in the lumber camps, often taking with them at least one of the older sons and the farm team, and returning to their farms just before the spring break-up. The cash wages they received were about a dollar a day for man and team, and that was a boon to the family finances, but it meant that the women and children left at home had to take full responsibility for the winter farm work, both inside and out. It must have been a lonely life, isolated by the heavy snows, responsible for keeping small children safe and well, with, in some cases, no horse in the stable to hitch up to go to call upon a neighbour or summon help.

Griddle for hearth cooking.
- PRIVATE COLLECTION

Pine wall box — once mended with shoe tacks and glazier's points, since rebroken.
- AUTHORS' COLLECTION

COOKING

During the nineteenth century in Canada a revolution was taking place in the kitchen as the cook stove gradually replaced the fireplace for cooking. It was a gradual process, but by the 1860s many homes, even in the rural areas, had a wood-burning cook stove installed in an old fireplace opening. New homes were being built without a kitchen fireplace, having been designed for a stove with pipes leading into a chimney. The disappearance of open hearth cooking changed the life of the cook for it meant that there was a safe and level spot on which to place cooking utensils, that the kitchen was no longer chronically smoky and coated with a film of ashes, and that the temperature at which foods were cooked was controllable to a greater extent. About June the cook stove could be moved out to the summer kitchen and moved back after the fall preserving had been completed. Those who could afford it put an old cookstove permanently in the summer kitchen and avoided the whole horrendous task of moving stove and pipes. The pipes, however, still had to be cleaned periodically, wherever the stove was located.

The first cook stoves seem low and awkward to us today, but this was no hardship to women used to bending down to cook on a hearth. For some time too, the thrifty housewife continued to use her heavy iron cooking vessels if they had flat bottoms, and these were easier to lift to a low stove top. Gradually tinware replaced some of the iron pots, and some stoves could be bought with a set of tin cooking pots.

One of the most onerous tasks of the farm wife was the preparation of three substantial meals a day for a large number of people. A household might consist of children of assorted ages, relatives who made their home with the family, and any hired labour the family could afford. Anyone who dropped in near meal time was pressed to stay, and travelling pedlars or circuit-riding preachers spent the night at the nearest home as darkness approached. Everyone old enough to work performed hard physical labour and therefore required three hearty meals. Farm horses were needed for the essential work in the fields, so people were in the habit of walking great distances, carrying heavy loads both going and returning. Breakfast on the farm was served usually after the men had done the outside chores. Dinner was the heaviest meal of the day and was served at noon, and supper was usually dinner warmed over, with the addition of sauces and pickles to liven it up. Salt pork and potatoes might appear three times a day, and often dessert was both pie and cake. When a barn-raising bee was held, a farm wife, with the help of her daughters and neighbouring women, sometimes served two meals to as many as 100 men. At one Ottawa Valley bee the menu served included beef, veal, mutton and pork, potatoes, bread and buns, cakes, puddings and pies, tea, coffee and whisky, plus assorted pickles and sauces.

Tin coffee pot.
- PRIVATE COLLECTION

Characteristic tinware — l. to r. clockwise: spice box; dipper; pie plate; apple corer; grater; moulds; funnel; cookie cutter.
- AUTHORS' COLLECTION

MEAT

Slaughtering usually took place in the early winter to provide natural refrigeration for the meat not to be used immediately, and to avoid having to winter the animals destined for slaughter. Beef was not frequently used for meat, as cattle were raised for dairy products and as work animals. Beef, when eaten, would usually come from an animal past its prime, and therefore was rather tough. Similarly, sheep were raised for wool and not primarily for mutton. Pigs were the only animal raised for food alone, and were usually penned and fed on corn and kitchen scraps.

The men did the actual slaughtering and cutting up of the carcasses outside, while in the house the women boiled the head and hocks for head cheese, and cooked the edible entrails. The small intestines were turned inside out and washed to be used as a casing for the sausages. To make the sausage filling the prime scraps were placed in a wooden bowl and cut up with a cutter with a convex steel blade. For those who could afford it a cast iron meat grinder was available by the mid-nineteenth century. After the usual seasoning of pepper and sage had been added, the meat was forced into the casing with a hand-operated sausage stuffer. The intestine was pulled over the narrow end of a tin sheath and the stuffing forced into it by a wooden plunger. A more complicated stuffer consisted of a heavy cast iron tube

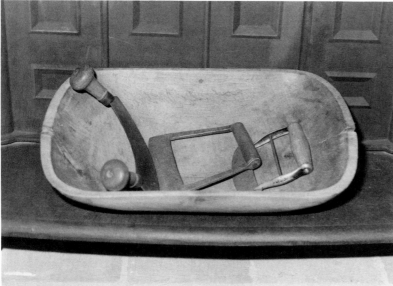

Rectangular wooden chopping bowl and convex cutters, centre cutter made from an old rasp. - AUTHORS' COLLECTION

Cast iron meat chopper.
- AUTHORS' COLLECTION

with an iron lever attached to the top with a hinged piston, which forced the meat into the casing.

The sausages, bacon, hams and shoulders which were to be smoked were packed in dry salt or a brine solution to be removed to the smoke house in about six weeks. The pork to be kept for family use or for sale was packed in barrels and covered with liquid brine. A barrel of salt pork weighed approximately 90 kilograms (200 pounds). Beef when salted was called pickled or corned beef.

The last job left, and apparently one that the women found rather difficult, was the making of lard. The fat to be rendered was cut into small pieces and slowly melted in the kettle. Too much heat would scorch the lard and make it useless. Small amounts of water were added to the fat to prevent it scorching on the bottom of the rendering kettle. With a wood paddle the pieces were squeezed against the side of the pot to separate the fat from the fibre. Finally, a hinged wooden lard press was used to separate the last pockets of fat from the fibrous parts, and the liquid was strained into stoneware jars which were covered and stored in a cool place. Good lard was said to keep in perfect condition for a year.

Sausage stuffer.

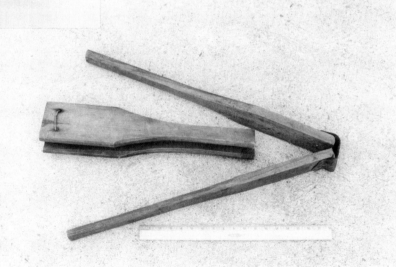

Hinged wooden lard presses.

FISH AND GAME

Fish, whether caught for sport or for food, added variety to daily meals. Even suckers were regarded as edible. Fish was eaten fresh, or preserved by drying, freezing or salting. Game also helped to break the monotony of the common diet of salt pork. Deer, moose, bear, raccoon, hare and black squirrels were eaten. Passenger pigeons were still to be found in great numbers and were roasted, cooked in pigeon pie, or salted or frozen for later use. They were fattest in the fall after having feasted on the farmer's grain.

POULTRY

Chickens were raised for the production of eggs rather than for eating. Roast chicken was a special treat because chickens past their prime were usually boiled. If water was nearby, geese and ducks were raised. Several times a year a stocking was pulled over the heads of the geese and they were plucked to provide down for mattresses and pillows. Geese and ducks were also used for roasting. Turkeys were less common than chickens and were not found on every farm. Children were usually responsible for feeding the poultry and gathering the eggs. Money from the sale of eggs and butter traditionally belonged to the farm wife.

BREAD

Bakeries had been established in larger centres by this time, but most rural and many town women baked all of the family's bread, an almost daily task in a large family. "Barm" or rising for bread was advertised for sale by breweries, but many farm women grew hops to make their own "hop rising." The ripe hop cones were boiled and the strained liquor was added to flour. When the mixture had cooled to lukewarm, a little brewer's yeast, or some old barm, was mixed in. This was covered and stored in a cool place. To provide hops for making rising in winter the cones were picked in late summer and dried.

The farmer took his grain to the closest grist mill and the miller would keep part of the flour as payment. The ground flour was often far from pure, and most households had a sieve for straining flour, as well as salt and white sugar. The bread dough was mixed in a large wooden bowl or in the dough box, using a wooden spoon or paddle. It was kneaded on a wooden dough board or on the lid of the dough box, turned upside down for this purpose. Some dough boxes had legs and some were made to sit on a table. They were usually made of pine and could be crudely formed or examples of the craftsman's art. Those made in Quebec were more likely to be carved and decorated. All had lids to protect the rising dough from the drafts of early kitchens. Where brick or clay bake ovens were still in use, the long handled wooden peel would be used to remove the cooked loaves.

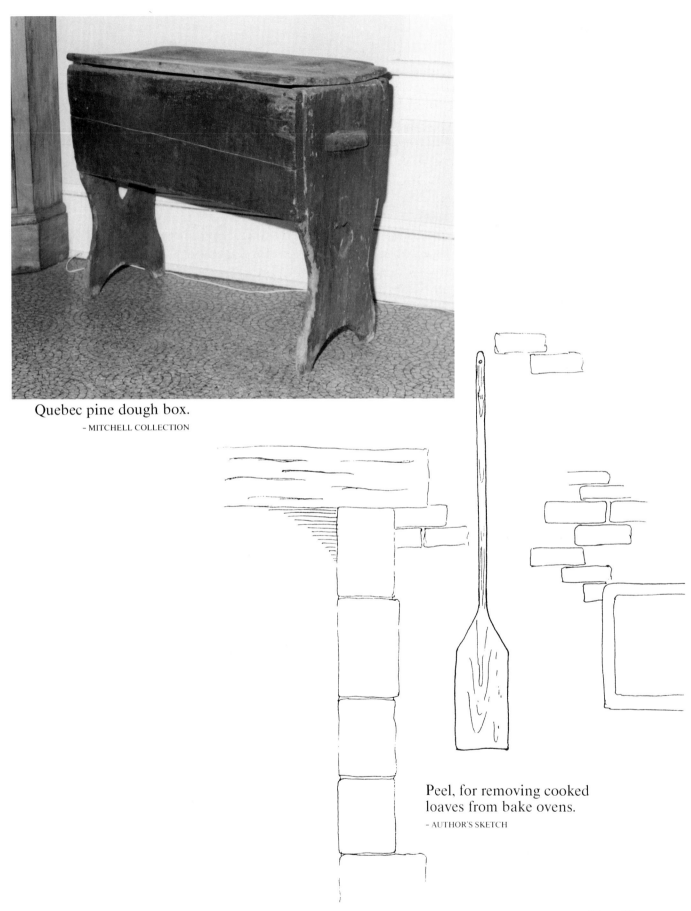

Quebec pine dough box.
— MITCHELL COLLECTION

Peel, for removing cooked
loaves from bake ovens.
— AUTHOR'S SKETCH

VEGETABLES

The kitchen garden was the responsibility of the women and children. The men did the original clearing and fencing, but the planting, weeding and watering were all parts of the household chores. Hardware trade catalogues of the day show a wide range of garden rakes, hoes, watering cans and so forth, but much of the gardening was probably done with basic tools, sometimes blacksmith-forged.

The variety of vegetables grown by the 1860s is quite surprising to us. Potatoes were a staple, but there were peas, sweet corn, beets, turnips, parsnips, carrots, broccoli, cauliflower, cucumbers, spinach, beans, onions, squash, lettuce, radishes, cabbage, pumpkins, tomatoes, asparagus and melons. Vegetables were not often served raw, and old cook books recommended boiling them for long periods. There were many different types of wooden mashers for vegetables. Turnips, pumpkins and cabbage were eaten by both humans and animals.

One common way of preserving cabbage for winter use was to make it into sauerkraut. The cabbage was cut up with homemade shredders constructed of wood with a metal cutting edge, often made from old knife or scythe blades, set into it. The shredder was placed over a barrel or crock so that the cabbage fell into it, and salt was spread between each layer. When the crock was full the contents were tamped down with a long-handled wooden beetle or pounder, covered with a board, and weighted down with a stone to keep the cabbage under the liquid brine which would be produced. Pumpkins were used fresh, or dried like apples for future use.

Cabbage slicer. - AUTHORS' COLLECTION

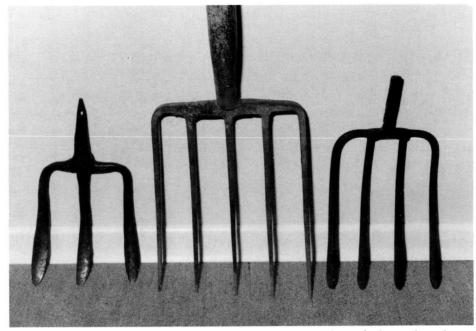

Three forks — hand-forged garden fork on left; centre and right factory-made garden forks.

Three wooden tampers.

FRUITS

The most universally used fruit was the apple, by now well established in Canadian orchards. They were often eaten raw, being kept in barrels in cellars as far into the winter as possible, but many were dried for longer preservation. Paring bees were held in the fall, and, like husking bees, were mostly for the young of courting age. The boys tried to turn up with the cleverest type of apple peeler. There were many wooden varieties, some decorated and even signed. Others were made of cast iron. Some fastened to table tops and some were mounted on a board so that the user sat on one end as he operated it. Most were quite ingenious, some coring as well as peeling. As the boys peeled the apples, the girls cored and sliced them, and they were threaded on strings and hung up in the kitchen. When dry they were stored in bags and when needed for pies or applesauce, they had only to be soaked in water and cooked.

Top and bottom: Apple peelers.
– BLOCKHOUSE MUSEUM, MERRICKVILLE

Cast iron lemon squeezer. - AUTHORS' COLLECTION

Wild fruits were picked in season, and eaten fresh or made into pies. Berry picking was left to the women and children, and strawberries, raspberries, choke-cherries, blueberries, blackberries, elderberries, high bush cranberries and wild plums could all be found. A berry picker, used most often for blueberries, was made of wood or metal with a comb-like mouth to strip the berries from the bushes, and a receptacle into which they fell. Berries were dried on screens in the sun, or made into preserves, jams, jellies and sauces. Glass and stoneware jars were used to store preserves.

The age of kitchen gadgetry had arrived, and there were many different types of cherry pitters to be found on the market as well.

Lemons could be purchased but were considered a luxury. Lemon squeezers were hinged presses made of wood or cast iron.

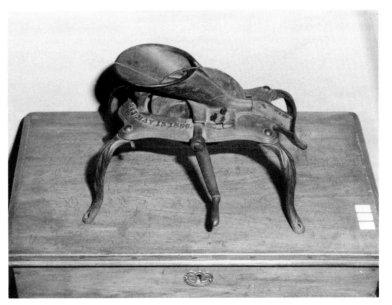

Cherry pitter.
- GRIPSHOLM ANTIQUES

Blueberry picker. - NATIONAL MUSEUMS OF CANADA NEG. 82-8140

DESSERTS

Cakes and muffins were often baked, using cream of tartar and baking soda purchased at the store as a rising. In old cook books instructions are quite vague, such as "butter the size of an egg," or a "handful" of this and that. Pies were popular, with more than one kind often served at one meal. Rhubarb was so often used it was called "pie plant" and apple and pumpkin were also favourites. For rolling out pastry the housewife used rolling pins made from a solid piece of wood, the most prized being those of figured maple. Some were carefully hand-crafted and others turned out in factories. The pastry was rolled out on the kitchen table or on a dough board. Puddings were boiled or steamed rather than baked, and for special occasions, such as Christmas, currants, raisins and peel could be bought. Ice cream freezers were for sale, consisting of a sheet metal container inside a wooden one, with a space for crushed ice mixed with salt in between. Through the tight-fitting lid of the inner cylinder ran a shaft which was turned by a crank, and ended in vertical paddles. Since the harvesting of ice was a cold and difficult task, ice was used with care, and ice cream regarded as a special treat.

Baking utensils — l. to r.: cake mould; grater; nutmeg grater; head cheese mould; cast iron muffin pan; wooden pastry crimper; (pastry board at rear).

Hand-crafted rolling pins. - AUTHORS' COLLECTION

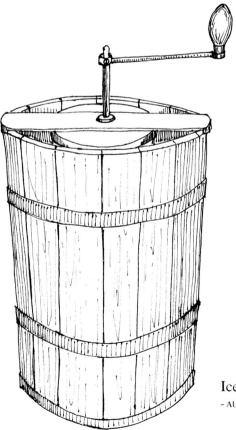

Ice cream freezer.
- AUTHOR'S SKETCH

Confederation kitchen — coffee mill at rear.
- UPPER CANADA VILLAGE, MORRISBURG

BEVERAGES

Individual farmers made apple cider. On some farms the buttermilk left over from churning was regarded as a fine drink, and on others it was fed to the pigs. Green tea was the common hot beverage in the Valley. Letters and diaries call the inhabitants "terrible" tea drinkers. It was served three times a day in the logging shanties, often stewed for hours on the stove. However tea was expensive, and substitutes were made of plants and trees found in the woods, such as New Jersey Tea and Labrador Tea, sassafras and hemlock, and herbs such as mint, sage and thyme. Coffee was imported in the form of green beans and had to be roasted and ground at home. Coffee roasters came in many forms, all made of tinware, for use on top of a stove. There was always some of moveable drum turned by hand to keep the beans from scorching. An ordinary frying pan agitated by hand was probably often used. Coffee grinders or mills also came in many styles. Box mills consisted of a metal grinding mechanism set into a wooden box. The coffee when ground fell down into a drawer which was then pulled out and emptied. Cast iron grinders which fastened to the wall for convenience were available at this time. Coffee, too, was expensive, and substitutes such as peas, wheat, barley, acorns and dandelion roots were ground up and roasted. Their use must have been fairly widespread as several of the grinders advertised for sale state that they will also grind coffee substitutes.

VINEGARS

Vegetables that were not to be preserved in root cellars could be pickled in the fall. Home-made vinegars were made from the last run of the maple sap by boiling it down to one-fifth of its volume, adding some barm and letting it stand in a warm place for several weeks. Apple cider exposed to the air for at least a month made a cider vinegar. Vegetables most often pickled were cucumbers, beans, cabbage and onions. Pickles were usually packed in stoneware jars.

SEASONINGS

Spices and herbs were an important part of pioneer cooking, both to add flavour and to cover up excess saltiness or spoilage. Most women grew a variety of herbs in their kitchen gardens to use for cooking and for medicinal drinks and poultices. Nutmeg, cinnamon, cloves and ginger were imported in their whole form. To use them the nutmeg and ginger had to be grated, and the cinnamon and cloves pounded in a wood mortar with a wooden pestle. These would also be used to crush the garden herbs. Larger graters were usually home-made, produced by piercing tin and bending it into a convex shape and fastening it to a piece of wood. Old tin pierced lanterns could be re-cycled into graters. Because nutmeg was grated in such small quantities, it required a small grater which was usually purchased. Every farm auction seems to provide evidence that nutmeg graters in several styles were almost always to be found in the rural kitchen.

Pantry with oak barrel; wash tub; grain measures; wooden shovel; covered
containers and storage jars.   – BELLEVUE HOUSE NATIONAL HISTORIC PARK, KINGSTON

Salt was imported in the form of rock salt, which had to be dried, pounded and
sifted. The salt box, a wooden container with a lid, hung near the stove to keep the
contents dry. Large quantities of salt were used in pickles, in butter making and in
brine for meats. Because butter and meat both tended to be salty, old recipes
generally do not call for the addition of salt. Pepper came in whole grains and had to
be pounded or ground. It was used in cooking but had yet to make its appearance on
the dinner table.

Because both brown and white sugar were imported and expensive, Valley
farmers often made their own maple sugar or bartered with neighbours who did. By
1854 Redpath had opened its first sugar refinery in Montreal, but the price was high
so it was reserved for special occasions. White sugar reached the general store in
conical loaves from which the storekeeper cut off a piece for the customer with sugar
shears. In the home this large hard piece was cut into smaller pieces with sugar
nippers, and these pieces were used whole or crushed and sieved. Honey was also
used as a sugar substitute, harvested from the farmer's own hives or obtained from a
neighbour.

Milking stool. - AUTHORS' COLLECTION

Dairy utensils — milkpans; handpierced sieve; dairy thermometer.
- AUTHORS' COLLECTION

BUTTER

Almost every farm family kept at least one cow to provide milk and butter. It was the job of the women and children to keep the family supplied with butter, and any that was not needed at home could be bartered at the general store, or sold for cash at the market in Ottawa. Mr. Alpheus Todd, the Parliamentary Librarian kept two cows in the city in 1864. This was not at all unusual as there was no milk delivery in Ottawa, and many town dwellers kept a cow to supply their own families. For their butter they counted on the farmers who lived nearby. The merchants who had shops along Wellington Street were spared having to keep their own cows because an enterprising Mrs. Keenahan delivered milk to them in their homes above their shops, charging five cents for 1.1 litres (one quart).

On the Valley farm the cows were milked twice a day and the milk was taken to the cellar or spring house where it was strained into glass, ceramic or metal containers to cool as quickly as possible. When the cream had risen to the surface it was removed with a skimmer, and stored until there was enough from several days milking to justify a churning. Sour cream churned better than sweet. Among the several kinds of churns were swing, rocker, barrel and box, but the most commonly used was the upright wooden or stoneware churn. This had a tightly fitting lid with a wooden rod which passed down through it and ended in a wooden cross. This rod or dasher was thrust up and down by the operator while in a standing position, agitating the cream in the container until it separated into solid lumps of butter and liquid buttermilk. This was a tedious process which could be affected by many factors, including the weather. Churning required a rhythmic motion, and this could be maintained by singing traditional butter-making songs. If anyone dropped in and found churning in process, it was considered wise not to engage the churner in conversation until the butter had "come." Often the children of the family helped in this part of the process.

After the lumps of butter had been formed, the buttermilk was drained off and saved for drinking or for the pigs. The butter was scooped out of the churn with wooden scoops and placed in a large round or rectangular or oval wooden bowl, and rinsed with cold water. It was then worked against the sides of the bowl with a wooden butter paddle until all possible moisture had been pressed out. It was rinsed again and worked at least once more. When it seemed that all liquid had been removed, salt was worked through the butter with the paddle, and if it appeared to be pale in colour it was sometimes tinted with yellow obtained from grated carrots, dandelion or marigold blossoms, or with a commercial butter tint. The best butter makers believed in one final rinse with more cold water, which had to be pressed out yet once more.

Some farmers made a special butter-worker for their wives. It was a triangular table with sides, the top being sloped down to the point of the triangle, and ending in a hole through which was pivoted a wooden bar with flat sides and a handle. The

Above: Upright churn — ceramic.
Left: Upright churn — wooden.

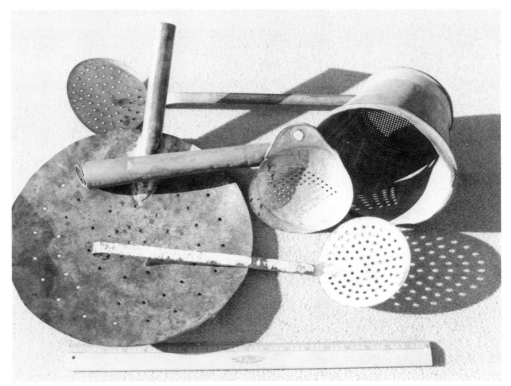

Collection of skimmers. - AUTHORS' COLLECTION

Home butter-maker's utensils — clockwise: stoneware pitcher; redware milk bowl; wooden butter bowl and paddle; assorted butter moulds; Scotch hands; butter crock. - AUTHORS' COLLECTION

Butter workers. - AUTHORS' COLLECTION

butter was taken from the churn and placed on the table part and the moisture squeezed out by rolling the bar in the arc of a circle, forcing the liquid to run down and out an opening in the narrow end. Butter was washed, rinsed, salted and coloured with more convenience than by using bowl and paddle.

However it was made, the secret of good butter was careful handling of the milk, complete removal of buttermilk, even colouring and the right amount of salt. Butter to be stored was packed in wooden pails or stoneware crocks, a cloth was spread over it and fine salt poured in to a depth of about 1 centimeter (½ inch). Paper was tied over all. Butter treated in this fashion would last for many months, and was easily transported. Smaller amounts were measured in wooden molds holding .4 or .8 kilograms (1 or 2 pounds). As it was forced out of the mold, the carved plunger imprinted a decorative pattern on the top surface. Because butter from different farms varied from good to almost inedible, depending on the diet of the cattle and the care taken in the making, a certain pattern could be used by the purchaser to identify the product from a certain farm which had established a reputation for excellence. Small carved butter prints were used to stamp butter to make it attractive for table use. Butter molds were at first hand-carved but later many were factory-made. Scotch hands were small rectangular ribbed bats used to form butter into balls for the table by rolling a small amount between the bats in a circular motion. They were also used to shape bulk butter scooped from a large container into a rectangular block.

CHEESE

The making of cheese was more complicated than the making of butter. For the production of rennet, necessary in cheese making, the first stomach of a sucking calf was saved at the time of slaughtering, cleansed carefully inside and out and soaked in brine for about 12 hours. It was then thoroughly dried and preserved in dry salt until needed.

At cheese-making time milk was placed in a tub and brought to blood temperature by the addition of warmed milk. To this milk was added a solution of dried rennet soaked in water, and the mixture was left to stand until a curd was formed. Then with a cheese knife or cutter of some kind the curd was cut lengthwise and crosswise to let the whey or liquid separate from the solid part of the curd. Next the curd was broken with the hands until it subsided under the whey. Some of the whey was then scooped from the tub and placed on the stove to heat slowly, and the curd was broken into smaller pieces with the hands and the heated whey returned to the tub. The process of heating the whey and returning it to the curd mixture was continued until the mixture in the tub reached a temperature of 36.7°C (98°F). At that point the contents of the tub were left for about half an hour and then stirred with a wooden paddle until the curd became firm. When the curds could be squeezed firmly in the hand and remain elastic and not stick together they were ready to be strained through a cheese basket lined with cloth. The dry curds were then returned to the original tub and about 100 grams (4 ounces) of salt added to each 4.5 kilograms (10 pounds) of curd, and the whole well mixed. The salted curd was packed into a cloth-lined wooden hoop and placed in a press. This could be as simple as two boards, one on top of the hoop and one on the bottom, with a heavy stone weighing down the top board, or a screw press which could be adjusted to provide increasing pressure. After two to four hours the cheese was turned and then left in the press until the next morning when it was removed, sprinkled with salt and set aside to cure in a cool cellar, being turned from time to time, and examined for mould. It would be considered ready for eating in about three to four weeks. Cheese made in this way was for family use, and was seldom really aged, being used within months.

By the 1860s the concept of the co-operative cheese factory had reached Canada from New York State where it originated. It proved to be a much more efficient way of making cheese and marketing it and enabled Valley farmers to deliver their milk to a factory which they managed themselves and in whose profits they all shared. Farmers could provide enough cheese for their own use and for export, and Canadian cheese soon was making a name for itself abroad.

Curd sieve.
- NATIONAL MUSEUMS OF CANADA NEG. 82-8141

Cheese press (screw) this one has been modified with a log head to be used alternatively as a house jack.
- AUTHORS' COLLECTION

Wooden laundry tub and dolly. – LENNOX AND ADDINGTON COUNTY MUSEUM, NAPANEE

Potash leach for soap-making — hollowed stump in lieu of barrel;
cauldron and cooler for boiling soap.

– UPPER CANADA VILLAGE, MORRISBURG

FIGHTING DIRT

For both the urban and rural housewife at this date the task of keeping her home, her family and their clothing in a state of reasonable cleanliness was a never-ending battle. Quantities of water had to be pumped, carried and heated, and disposed of after use. In Ottawa there was no waterworks system until 1875 and water came from private or communal wells, or was delivered from the Ottawa River in horse-drawn water carts and paid for by the barrel.

SOAP MAKING

Soap could be bought or bartered for in the general store, but many thrifty countrywomen made their own. Farm soap was a chemical compound produced by boiling fat with lye. Waste kitchen fats were rendered down and stored in a fat box or barrel, to be augmented by those fats from the late fall slaughter that were not suitable for tallow or lard. Hardwood ashes were stored in the ash house or other dry place. Spring was the best time to make the year's supply of soap since the whole odorous job could be performed outside, and there would be less fat to be stored over the hot summer period.

To produce the lye, or "ley", a barrel with a hole drilled in the bottom was placed on a raised platform which was tilted slightly forward so that the liquid lye would run out the hole and down a wooden trough into a container. A layer of twigs was placed at the bottom of the barrel and then a layer of straw. The ashes were put in alternately with layers of lime, and all was tamped down with a long-handled wooden pounder. Hot water was poured in at the top of the barrel, and cold soft water added from time to time. Within a day or two a dark red liquid began to run from the barrel and collect in the container. As soon as the liquid began to run a little paler, the lye was tested for strength. An egg was placed in the solution and, if it floated just enough to show a portion the size of a small coin, the lye was just the right potency. If the egg rose higher it meant that the solution was too strong, and water was added slowly until the egg sank to the proper level.

The rendered fat was heated in a large cauldron, while being stirred continuously with a long-handled wooden paddle, and the lye was added slowly. The mixture was then boiled over a small, steady fire, stirred constantly and closely supervised, so that if too much greasy foam rose to the surface more lye could be added, or if no grease showed at all, more fat could be poured in. When the mixture thickened it was poured into crocks or tubs to be used as soft soap. This could be scooped out by hand or by a home-made wooden scoop with a handle. If hard soap was to be made, the soft mixture was boiled for a longer period and several handfuls of salt stirred in. It was then left to cool overnight and the solid cake which had formed on top was removed and boiled with turpentine or resin, and more salt. The resulting mixture was poured into a wooden box lined with cloth, and when it had hardened was lifted out and cut into bars. Hard soap improved with age if stored in a dry place.

The making of soap was a hit-or-miss affair. Because the quality of the fat and ashes, the strength of the lye, the size of the pot and the heat of the fire all varied so much, recipes giving relative amounts of fat and lye were almost useless. Some women just seemed able to produce better soap than others. A number of superstitions grew up around the process, such as the necessity of stirring in one direction only, and choosing the right phase of the moon for the boiling. Not surprisingly it was the custom to wish good luck to anyone about to embark on this laborious and uncertain process.

LAUNDERING

Whenever possible, soft water was used for washing clothes as the harsh home-made soap lathered much better in rain or river water. This meant that the weather and the amount of water available had often more to do with the day chosen for the washing than the number of clothes needing laundering. Hard soap, if available, was preferred to the soft for laundering, and was slivered and dissolved in hot water.

The washing process was easier if clothes were soaked overnight. The next day all the water had to be carried in wooden pails and heated on the stove. Piggins, which were wooden containers with one slat left longer to serve as a handle, were used as dippers. The wooden wash tubs, which had lugs for lifting, were placed on a low wash bench, and the clothes were scrubbed in warm water with wooden wash boards which had wooden or zinc scrubbing bars. Another form of washer was a wooden hand-cranked affair resembling a wringer, but with corrugated wooden rollers instead of smooth ones. When clothes were run through this device several times, the same scrubbing effect was achieved as if a washboard had been used.

Wooden washboard with zinc scrubber.
- LYALL CLARKE COLLECTION

Advertisement. - PETERSON'S MAGAZINE, 1870

Another method was to place a tub of soapy water on the floor and agitate the clothes by plunging a long-handled wooden dolly up and down, as in a dash churn. The base of the dolly was shaped to give maximum suction action. After scrubbing, the cottons and linens were boiled in a metal pot on the stove while being stirred with a wooden laundry stick or with wooden tongs. Wringers, cranked by hand and equipped with wooden or rubber rollers, were in common use, but some women still wrung their clothes by hand.

After rinsing, white clothes normally were blued in a solution of indigo which had to be purchased, and those to be starched were stiffened with home-made starches concocted from potatoes or bran. Corn starch could be purchased, but it was expensive, and was more likely to be used in cooking. The clean clothes were carried to the clothesline in splint or willow baskets, and hung up with hand-whittled wooden pegs. Spring clothes pins were available for those who could afford them. The final washday task was to water the garden with the rinse water, and use the sudsy wash water to wash the veranda, back stoop or privy floor.

Except for the metal pot used to boil the clothes, most washday tools were made of wood, usually cedar, since it was best able to withstand constant wetting. These utensils would be crafted by a cooper, for this kind of work required expertise. Tubs, piggins and all waterproof containers were stored between usings with water in them so that they would not shrink and begin to leak.

Many families omitted one or more of the steps outlined, and whenever possible, shaking, sponging and airing took the place of washing as long as possible, especially in winter. In summer, laundering could be moved to the summer kitchen, or even outside. Wherever it took place the whole process was taxing, and even dangerous with so much boiling water being handled.

Wooden washer (two views).
– BLOCKHOUSE MUSEUM, MERRICKVILLE

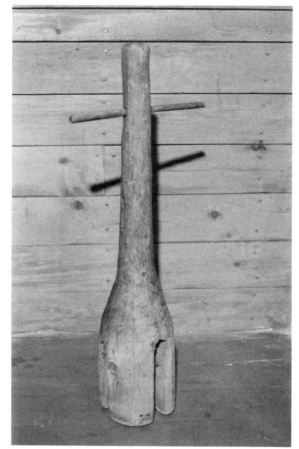

Wooden laundry tongs, wash stick and wash dolly. - AUTHORS' COLLECTION

Primitive wash dolly.
- BLOCKHOUSE MUSEUM. MERRICKVILLE

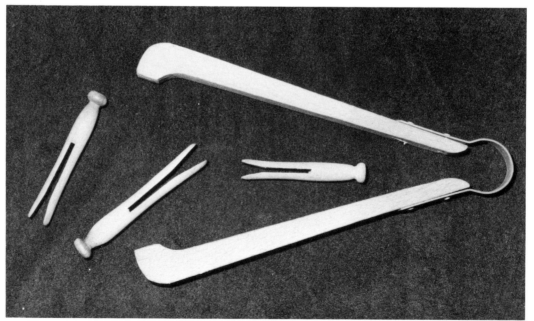

Factory-made clothes pegs and laundry tongs. - AUTHORS' COLLECTION

IRONING

As soon as stoves came into general use, they provided a flat and reasonably clean surface on which to heat sad irons. The origin of the word "sad" had no connection with mood, but meant "heavy", and this they certainly were. Several flat irons were heated at the same time, and as one cooled in use another would be substituted from the stove. Since the handle was cast as part of the iron, it too heated up, and had always to be grasped with a cloth pad. Around 1870, a woman named Mrs. Potts invented an iron with a wooden detachable handle, which could be transferred from a cooling base to a hot one, and did not conduct heat. It must have been a boon to those women lucky enough to own one.

The two-piece fluting iron consisted of a corrugated iron base which was heated, and a curved corrugated top, which was rocked to and fro over the garment to press crimped or pleated trim. The goffering iron was named from the French word "gaufrer" meaning "pleat". It was a hollow finger-shaped iron sheath mounted on a stand, and was heated by an iron rod which was warmed on the stove and thrust into the sheath. To press lace, frills or ribbons, they were pulled back and forth over the heated surface. These specialized irons were, of course, of use only to those who could afford them, and for many women the sad iron remained the only type available. Irons had to have iron stands to keep them from scorching the surface they were placed upon when not in use. These could be hand-forged or factory made, and the ones made in Quebec were often original and whimsical in form.

Ironing boards were exactly that, boards padded with an old blanket and covered with a piece of linen or cotton. They were narrower at one end and were usually placed between the backs of two kitchen chairs. Smaller boards, similarly shaped, with low stands suitable for use on a table top, were called sleeve boards. For many a Valley woman, however, the only ironing surface was one end of the kitchen table with an old blanket spread over it. Wooden clothes racks were used for indoor drying and for airing the clothes after ironing.

Sad iron; iron stand; detachable wooden-handled sad iron.

– LENNOX AND ADDINGTON COUNTY MUSEUM, NAPANEE

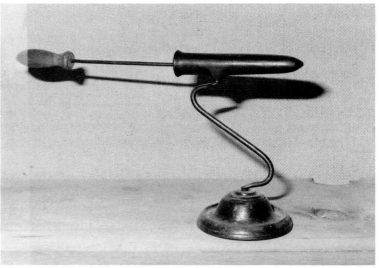

Goffering iron.
- LENNOX AND ADDINGTON COUNTY MUSEUM, NAPANEE

Ironing boards, regular and sleeve.
- AUTHORS' COLLECTION

Roller-type fluting iron.
- LENNOX AND ADDINGTON COUNTY MUSEUM, NAPANEE

Wooden drying or towel rack. - AUTHORS' COLLECTION

CLEANING THE HOUSE

With the first warm days of spring there was a frenzy of spring cleaning. Rugs were carried outside and beaten with carpet beaters made of wire or cane. Floors were swept and the old straw replaced with fresh before the rugs were again tacked down. Curtains and bedding were aired in the sun and walls and windows washed. Once this had been done, the routine tidying or "redding up" for the rest of the year was much the same in all rural homes.

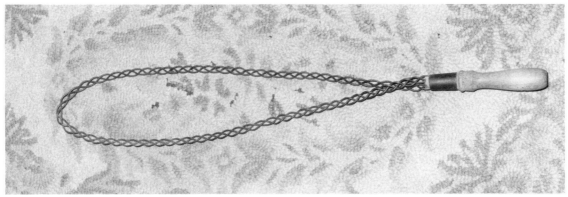

Carpet beater on hand-hooked rug. - AUTHORS' COLLECTION

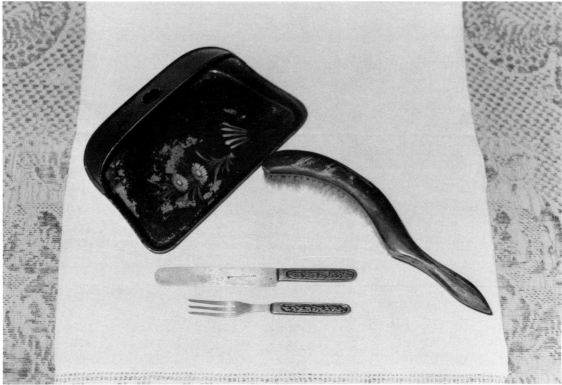

Steel-bladed cutlery with iron handles; tole crumb tray and brush.
- AUTHORS' COLLECTION

Dishes were washed after every meal. Steel-bladed cutlery had to be cleaned after every use, a job often done by the children. A wooden knife board hung on the wall, with a scouring brick stored in the wooden pocket at the base. This was laid flat on the table and the cutlery scoured on the back of the board itself. Since this was usually made of soft pine, most knife boards show a hollow worn by the cleaning process. Pots and pans were scoured with sand or ashes, although metal pot scrapers were now available. Floors were scrubbed on hands and knees, using a stiff brush and soft soap. Sometimes sand or a solution of lye was used to restore the lighter colour to pine floors. Small rugs could be shaken outside in summer or swept in the snow in winter, but large rugs were sprinkled with damp used tea leaves to keep down the dust, and swept with a broom. A carpet sweeper had been invented but it could be operated only in a forward motion, not back and forth.

Corn brooms could by this time be bought from broom makers or from the general store, but a splint broom could be made at no cost from a birch sapling, using only a jackknife. A description of the method is as follows:

First, an even layer of wood about 1 centimetre (½ in.) deep was removed from the lower 35 centimetres (14 in.) of a sapling about 1.5 metres (5 ft.) long *(a-b in diagram)*.

This section was split upward into a bundle of coarse fibres. A cut was then made about 40 centimetres (16 in.) up from the shredded core, about 1 centimetre (½ in.) deep, all around the sapling. The section *(c-d in diagram)* was then shredded downward into fibres.

The shredded section *(c-d)* was then pulled down over the shredded core, tied firmly, and all the fibres were trimmed to a common length. The handle *(e-f in diagram)* was then whittled to a suitable diameter and cut to the required length.

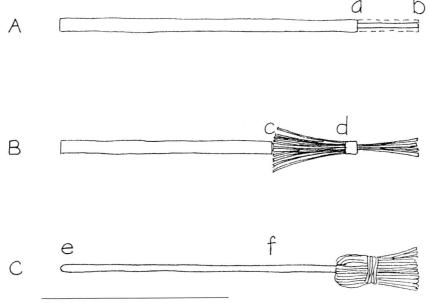

Splint broom. - AUTHOR'S SKETCH

After floors were swept, the contents of the wooden or metal dustpan were sorted through so that nothing as precious as a needle or a hairpin was thrown away. In the bedrooms, ticks and mattresses had to be turned and shaken every day, as feathers, straw and corn husks all tended to form lumps. A bed pole like a rather long rolling pin was used to smooth the ticks, but it is likely that most rural housewives substituted a broom handle. Every fall the straw and corn husks had to be taken from the ticks and replaced. The rope in rope beds stretched and let the mattresses sag, and so it had to be tightened from time to time with a wooden rope key. This is probably the source of the saying, "Good night, sleep tight, don't let the bedbugs bite."

Hearth (note splint broom).
– BLOCKHOUSE MUSEUM,
MERRICKVILLE

Pine knife board.
– PRIVATE COLLECTION,
MANOTICK

Rope key or rope wrench.
– AUTHORS' COLLECTION

The kerosene lamps and kitchen and parlour stoves which had brought advantages to the Valley women, after about 1860, brought also extra chores. Lamp chimneys had to be cleaned and polished after every use, and wicks had to be kept trimmed with lamp scissors. Stoves could be kept clean from day to day by brushing with a goose or turkey wing, but periodically they had to be blacked and polished. Ashes had to be shaken down and carried out, and twice a year there was no avoiding the ordeal of taking down the stove pipes, cleaning them outside, and putting them up again. The men of the family usually helped with this task, which from all accounts left everybody in a foul temper for some time.

Even if the parlour was not used often, it had still to be dusted and the furniture kept shining, and all those Victorian nick-nacks had to be looked after.

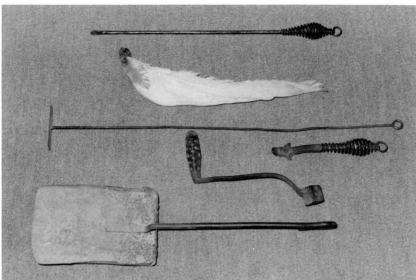

Stove tools — bottom to top: ash shovel; grate shaker; lid lifter; ash rake; goose wing; poker.
- AUTHORS' COLLECTION

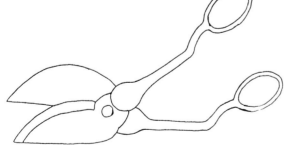

Wick trimmer. - AUTHOR'S SKETCH

Kerosene lamps — kitchen and parlour. - AUTHORS' COLLECTION

Shaving tools —
l. to r.: shaving mug;
hone; strop; razor.

PERSONAL CARE

The difficulties of carrying and heating water, plus the wintry chill of any room except the kitchen, made standards of personal cleanliness more casual than those of today. In summer a basin, pail and dipper rested on a bench outside the kitchen door, not too far from the well and rain barrel, with a container of soft soap and a communal towel. It was not unheard of to leave the soapy water for the next comer. In cold weather a bucket bench in the kitchen held pail, basin, soap and dipper, along with a pail of drinking water. Waste water was poured into a slop bowl or pail if there was no sink, and a kettle of hot water was always simmering on the stove. The men usually shaved in the kitchen also. The razor used would be a straight one, made of the finest steel, usually imported from Sweden or Britain. The handles were made of wood, bone, tortoise shell or ivory. The blades took an exceedingly sharp edge, which was maintained with a fine stone razor hone and a leather strop. Shaving brushes were generally of hog bristles or badger hair, mounted in a wooden handle, and a shaving mug held the soap cake needed to produce a lather.

Saturday night preparations for church-going on Sunday included bringing out the tin bath tub from its storage in the summer kitchen and filling it with water heated on the stove so that the weekly full bath could take place. A kettleful of hot water was added from time to time, and modesty was maintained by hanging sheets or blankets around the tub, and so, basically, the family shared even its bath water. For sponge baths or daily ablutions hot water could be carried upstairs to be used in ewers and basins, but few households without a servant or hired girl could manage such a luxury. The newly popular toilet sets included toothbrush holders and tooth glasses, and tooth brushes were listed for sale in stores, but it is difficult to be sure how widespread regular tooth brushing actually was.

Often a communal brush and comb were hung in a holder on the kitchen wall, accompanied by a mirror, to be used for a last minute grooming before leaving the house.

Great wheel. – UPPER CANADA VILLAGE. MORRISBURG

Carding boards, factory-made.

– LENNOX AND ADDINGTON COUNTY MUSEUM. NAPANEE

Treadle or Saxony wheel.

– UPPER CANADA VILLAGE. MORRISBURG

TEXTILES

SPINNING

As soon as the new settlers in the Valley had satisfied the most urgent need of providing a roof over their heads and planting food, they had to turn their thoughts to providing warm clothing to wear and coverings for their beds so that they could survive the cold winters. Immigrants who came as cabin passengers could bring a fair number of possessions with them, but the majority, who travelled steerage, could bring few extra clothes and often these were not suitable for their new environment and occupations. They had to turn sheep's wool into yarn and flax into linen by the process of spinning.

At first it was difficult to keep sheep because of the cold winters and the attacks of predators but, as animal shelters were built and the land cleared and fenced, most rural families were able to keep a few sheep to provide wool. Grey homespun was produced by mixing the wool of one black sheep with that of three white but the proportions could be altered to create the desired shade.

In the spring, as soon as the sheep no longer needed their heavy winter coats, they were washed in the nearest stream and confined to pasture for a couple of days to dry before being sheared. This was the responsibility of the farmer and older boys, but, at this point, they returned to the urgent job of spring planting and the rest of the process of turning raw wool into yarn was turned over to the women and younger children. The shorn fleeces were spread out on the grass in the shade to dry thoroughly and all burrs, twigs and matted wool were removed. Before the wool could be carded the natural oils had to be replaced by pouring melted oil, lard, or waste butter over the wool in proportions of about 1 kilogram (2.2 pounds) of grease to 3.6 kilograms (7.4 pounds) of wool. When this had been thoroughly worked in by hand, the softened wool was ready for carding.

By the 1860s those who lived near the many woollen mills already built could have the carding done in exchange for a portion of the finished product, but those who lived in isolated areas, and those who had still to count every penny, did the carding at home. Carding boards consisted of two rectangular pieces of board covered with leather on the inside, with handles set at right angles. The leather was studded with curved wire bristles. The carder sat holding one of the cards in the left hand, resting it on the knee, and placed a handful of raw wool on the upturned wire teeth. The other card was held in the right hand with the teeth facing downward, and was drawn repeatedly across the other board until all the strands of wool had been straightened and ran in the same direction. The carded wool was removed by reversing the action of the top card, so that the wool was pulled off the bottom card in a roll or roving. This might be set aside until there was time to spin it into yarn. Carding could provide a pleasant task for grandmother as she sat beside the stove in winter, as wool was more easily handled when warm.

The technique of spinning was known in most primitive societies and, although differing methods were employed, the principle remained the same: fibres were drawn out, twisted under tension, and the spun thread was wound up.

Spinning has always been particularly associated with the women of the family, and the female descent in genealogy is referred to as the "distaff" side. In Proverbs 31:13, when King Lemuel describes the virtuous woman, he says "She seeketh wool, and flax, and worketh willingly with her hands." And in 31:19 he adds "She layeth her hands to the spindle, and her hands hold the distaff."

The great wheel, or "muckle wheel" as it was known in Scotland, was used only for the spinning of wool. The spinner, in a standing position, twisted by hand a piece pulled from the roving, and fastened it to the end of the spindle. She then spun the wheel clockwise with her right hand and stepped back about three paces, holding the roving in her left hand and drawing out the fibre under tension. Next she turned the wheel counter-clockwise slowly, just until the spun yarn backed from the end of the spindle to the middle. Then she gave the wheel a spin in the original direction which wound the spun yarn on the spindle as she took about three paces forward. The action of the great wheel was intermittent, and thus suitable for spinning the soft fibre of wool. As the spinner went backward and forward she might walk 32 kilometres (20 miles) in the course of a day's spinning. In the soft pine floors of old houses, where the wheel was used in the same spot for many years, one sometimes can see paths worn by the feet of long-gone spinners as they pursued their repetitive task.

The small treadle wheel was much more complicated. The spinner was seated, and operated the treadle with her feet, since both hands were needed to spin flax. The fibres were carefully wrapped around the distaff and tied, and the distaff was placed on the standard which held it higher than the wheel. A small container to hold water was mounted on the frame or placed nearby to moisten the flax with the fingers, as it was more manageable when wet. The left hand directed the fibres from the distaff to the right hand, which fed them into the spindle, which revolved at a different rate than the bobbin. This meant that, unlike the great wheel, the motion was continuous, and that the fibre was wound up as it was spun. When the flax wheel was used for wool, the roving was held in the lap and fed directly into the spindle. This wheel was certainly more difficult to master but, since it could be used to produce both yarn and linen, it was a treasured possession. Some had been brought with the settlers when they came. Walking wheels usually were made locally and were quite basic, but many of the flax wheels brought to the Valley or constructed in the area were crafted with loving skill. In Quebec they were often painted in bright colours.

The last process in spinning is the winding of spun fibre. Whichever type of wheel was used, the yarn had to be removed from the spindle as soon as it interfered with the spinning process and arranged in a skein. One device used for this purpose was the niddy-noddy which was held in the centre with the left hand while the right hand guided the yarn around the arm. The rounds were counted as the niddy-noddy was twisted and turned in a rhythmic fashion until 40 rounds had been tallied. A more common and easily used winding and measuring device was the wool winder, usually containing a mechanism which made a clacking noise when 40 rounds had been wound, indicating that 73 metres (80 yards) of yarn were in the skein. It was important that the skeins should be of equal length to be assured of an even colour in the dyeing process. The skeins were washed and rinsed thoroughly, and hung in the shade to dry.

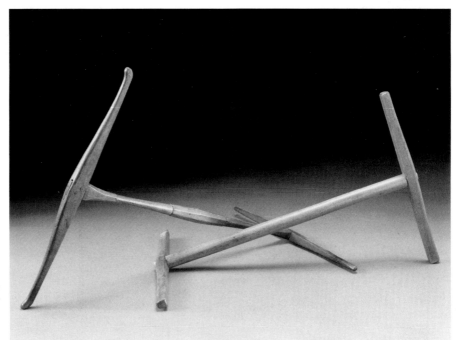

Two niddy-noddies.
- NATIONAL MUSEUMS OF
CANADA NEG. NO. 79-7431

Swift.
- BLOCKHOUSE MUSEUM, MERRICKVILLE

Wool winder.
- AUTHORS' COLLECTION

DYEING

The spun yarn could be, and often was, used in its natural colour, which could vary from off-white to dark brownish grey, depending upon the mixture of black and white wool. The pioneer women must have yearned for a way of brightening their drab surroundings for they learned from the native peoples, and by experimentation, how to colour their yarn by using trees and plants which grew all around them. Sumac and bittersweet produced orange; wild parsnip, horse radish, onion skins, marigolds and goldenrod fawns to yellows; black walnuts and buttercups gave browns, and blackberries purple. Some sacrifices were probably made to buy the expensive imported indigos and cochineals and primary colours were mixed experimentally to produce different shades.

The skeins of yarn to be dyed were dipped in soft water and then simmered in the dye solution long enough to produce the desired shade, usually at least an hour. Vegetable dyes had to have a mordant, such as alum or urine, added to the solution to "fix" the colour. While they simmered the skeins were stirred with wooden dye sticks which took on the colours of the dyes used, and can therefore be identified when found today. Iron pots were used in the dyeing of dark colours, but copper and tin containers were more successful for production of more delicate shades. Pleasing variations of the same colour could be achieved by braiding several skeins together before dyeing.

After removal from the solution the skeins had to be thoroughly rinsed again, and once more hung in the shade to dry. Since many unpleasant odours were generated in the dyeing process, it was best done outside and at some distance from the home.

For convenience in knitting, the yarn had to be wound into a ball. To do this the skein was placed on a swift which revolved as the skein was unwound but, being placed on a heavy base or fastened down in some way, left the user's hands both free to use in the winding process. Swifts varied in style from the finely crafted to some made from a suitably shaped crotch cut from a tree and mounted on a heavy wooden base.

FLAX

Flax was not grown extensively because its production and preparation was a complicated process, consisting of many steps, and involving much heavy and dirty work. The seeds were planted in early spring, sown thickly so that the plants would grow straight and tall. The women and children did the careful weeding which was essential and, just before the seed pods were completely ripe, the crop was harvested by pulling up each plant, root and all. These were then tied in bundles and piled in stooks to allow the seeds to ripen. To separate the seeds from the stalks, the sheaves were drawn through a large iron comb called a ripple, which was usually mounted on a bench so that the operator was seated. The seeds were saved for planting the following year. The stalks were then retted or rotted by immersion in soft water or by dew retting, which meant that they were spread thinly over the ground and exposed to rain and dew while being turned from time to time. This destroyed the bark and

Ripple.
- CANADA FARMER, 1865, NATIONAL MUSEUMS OF CANADA

Flax brake.
- CANADA FARMER, 1865
NATIONAL MUSEUMS OF CANADA

Heckle or hatchel.
- LENNOX AND ADDINGTON COUNTY MUSEUM, NAPANEE

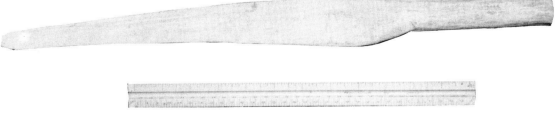

Scutching knife. - AUTHORS' COLLECTION

woody core, freeing the fibre which lay in between without damaging it. Water retting might take 10 days to 2 weeks. Dew retting depended upon the weather and was variable.

Next, the flax was dried, tied in bundles, and set aside until a suitable time arrived for braking and scutching. The brake was an arrangement of fixed wooden bars mounted on a frame, and a moveable wooden blade which was brought down repeatedly upon the bundle of flax as it was moved across the bars. This crushed the already rotted core, but left the fibres untouched. To remove the last of the broken stalks the flax was beaten against a log or board with a shaped piece of wood called a scutching knife or swingle. This left the fibre almost clean, but in a tangled state.

Up to this point the preparation of the flax had usually been done by the male members of the family, but now it was taken over by the women. The fibres were drawn through a heckle or hatchel, a wooden board fitted with teeth or spikes. The coarse or broken fibres which caught in the teeth were called "tow" and were used for rope or sacking. The long fibres came through straight and silky, ready to be spun into linen thread, which lacks the resiliency of wool, but is the strongest natural fibre.

WEAVING

Woven cloth consists of two series of fibres, with one series (the warp) running lengthwise and the other (the weft) running crosswise. Cloth is made on a loom. Whatever form it takes, the loom is the frame that holds the warp threads tightly and lowers and raises them so that the shuttle can be moved from one side to the other carrying the weft in between the warp threads.

It is not likely that many complete looms were brought to the Valley by settlers, as their bulk would have made them difficult to transport, but they did bring with them skill and technical knowledge of weaving which enabled them to build looms from local wood after they arrived. Looms were pegged together so that they could be taken apart and stored when not in use. Some weavers kept their looms in sheds and outbuildings, but that limited their use to times when the weather was suitable. Lucky indeed was the weaver who had a room or an attic in which the loom could be left up and ready to use whenever time and a supply of material to be woven was available. Shuttles were usually hand-made, and varied from crude to carefully shaped and polished. Some even had an added touch of inlay.

For everyday wear, cloth was usually woven with a linen warp and a wool weft, and was commonly known as linsey-woolsey. Cotton thread could be purchased at the general store or from a travelling pedlar and substituted for the linen warp to make a less scratchy cloth. For better clothing wool was used for both warp and weft, and by using coloured yarn in the weft, checks and stripes could be produced to make it even more pleasing. Woollen cloth which was to be used for warm outer wear was fulled to make it shorter, stronger and thicker. At one time this was done by a local bee but the result was not usually satisfactory, since large pieces of woollen cloth had to be soaked in soapy water and pulled, pushed and twisted by hands and even feet. By the middle of the nineteenth century almost all fulling was being done at a fulling mill in return for a proportion of the finished cloth.

Warm bedding and household linens were needed as well as clothing. Winter

Loom. - UPPER CANADA VILLAGE, MORRISBURG

sheets were woven of cotton and homespun, and blankets of wool warp and weft. Since the longest manageable distance that a shuttle could be thrown by hand from side to side was 75 centimetres (30 inches), this was the widest cloth available, and sheets, blankets and coverlets were made of strips sewn together. Towels and summer sheets were woven of pure linen. A coarser linen weave produced ticking for mattresses and pillows. Every housewife hoped to have at least one decorative woven coverlet, the most common combination of colours being blue and white.

The heddles that control the warp threads on a loom are strung on shafts or harnesses. The number of these harnesses determines what can be woven on a loom. Most Ontario looms had four harnesses, while the Quebec looms had two. This meant that weaving in each province developed a distinctive style. Because of this mechanical limitation the Quebec weavers developed hand-patterning to a fine art.

The hand loom was used in Quebec to produce the famous long fringed sashes known as "ceintures fléchées" because of their arrowhead motifs. They were woven lengthwise with basic colours of red, white and blue, with red predominating, and were worn by men of all classes.

Shuttle.
- LENNOX AND ADDINGTON COUNTY
MUSEUM, NAPANEE

QUILTING

Quilting is an ancient art, consisting of taking two lengths of material which in themselves have no particular warmth, and, by sewing them together with a lining of cotton or wool, producing a warm covering.

A little girl usually started about the age of eight to make the tops of the quilts she would need for her trousseau. There were basically two types: pieced, which were made of scraps of material sewn together for a top, or appliquéd, which were made out of whole cloth and had colour and interest added by sewing or appliquéing scraps of old or new material to the top. The quilting bee was a wonderful way to get together with other neighbourhood women and exchange patterns, quilt scraps and news, while stitching the top, bottom and lining of a quilt together with small even stitches, ideally about nine to the inch.

The quilt to be joined together was fastened in a frame generally made of 2.5 by 5 centimetres (1 by 2 inches) or 2.5 by 8 centimetres (1 by 3 inches) pine strips about 2.4 metres (8 feet) long. It could be adjusted to fit the quilt and then locked into position at the four corners using cast-iron or hand-forged wrought iron clamps. The frame rested on the back of four straight chairs and the quilters sat around the frame, not more than eight being able to work efficiently on one quilt. When the stitching was complete the edges were finished with a binding.

Quilting bees were usually held in the afternoon. The men and boys arrived at supper time, and the evening usually ended with a dance. Traditions grew up around quilting, and beautiful regional patterns were created. After a bridal quilting bee in some areas it was customary to catch the prospective groom and toss him in the newly completed quilt. In another part of the Valley the family cat was thrown into the middle of the quilt while it was still on the frame, and the closest unmarried girl to the spot where it made its escape supposedly would be the next bride.

Clamps for quilting frame. - AUTHORS' COLLECTION

Quilting frame. - MARGUERITE SUNNUCK COLLECTION

RUGS

The new large houses had cold bedroom and parlour floors to be covered. Imported rugs were available, but few people in rural areas could afford the high prices. Woven rag rugs were an attractive substitute, and could be made at home with rags and a loom. It took some time to collect enough rags, but every scrap was saved, cut or torn into strips, joined together and rolled into large balls. Even quite young children could be taught to do this task. White strips were usually dyed before use because they showed the dirt too soon. A cotton warp was used and the rags provided the weft. A special longer shuttle designed to hold the thick weft of rags was employed. Colours could be picked at random or wound separately onto balls of the same colour to produce a planned pattern. Another kind of hand-woven carpet was called drugget and was made of dyed wool yarn for warp with hemp or cotton weft. When woven only the warp showed, producing longitudinal stripes of various colours. If not used as mats these strips were sewn together and used as wall-to-wall carpets, being placed over a padding of straw. Carpet stretchers with a row of teeth to hold the carpet and a lever to stretch it were used, and the edges tacked down. By 1865 a combination carpet stretcher and tacker could be purchased. The home-woven carpeting was warm and attractive, and observation of the pieces that have survived shows the colours as still surprisingly fresh and bright.

The braided rug was the simplest to make. The prepared rags were braided into a rope and sewn into oval or circular shapes. One of their advantages was that they could be made larger at any time if the need arose.

The hooking of rugs is also an ancient art. A piece of burlap, linen or other closely woven material was stretched on a frame similar to that used in quilting, but smaller in size. The pattern was outlined on the material and rags or yarn were pulled through in a loop, using a rug hook made from metal, wood or bone. The hooks could be elaborately made, or as simple as a bent nail set into a wooden handle. The pattern was usually set off by a solid coloured border. Hooked rugs made in Quebec tended to represent animals, scenes or religious symbols, while Ontario rugs were more apt to be geometric or floral in design.

Carpet stretchers. - AUTHORS' COLLECTION

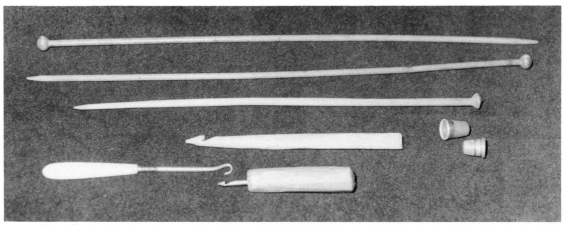

Textile tools plus button hook — whittled knitting needle
(centre); hand-made rug hooks. - AUTHORS' COLLECTION

KNITTING

If yarn was to be used for weaving, a single strand was sufficient, but if for knitting, it was usually strengthened by spinning several strands together. Two or three strands were fed onto the spindle and the wheel was turned counter-clockwise, twisting the yarn onto two or three ply. Knitting was an essential skill for women in the Valley. Little girls learned to knit early, and no woman sat down with empty hands, for a steady stream of socks, stockings, underwear, mittens, shawls, sweaters and head-coverings had to be produced to clothe the family. All that was required were needles and yarn, and anything knitted that a family did not use could be bartered or sold. Knitting was portable too, and could be carried when visiting.

STRAW WORK

Oats, wheat and rye were used for straw work, cut before the grain ripened completely, and stored until it could be used. The stalks were first soaked, then braided into coils while still wet and pliable. These coils were then flattened in a straw press. Hats for men, women and children were made by shaping them on a wooden hat form, starting at the crown. If no hat form was available a kitchen bowl could be substituted, and an imaginative woman could decorate her hat to suit her fancy. Braids could also be made into belts, mats or even small rugs.

CROCHETING AND TATTING

Crocheted articles usually were not essentials, but something to decorate the home. The only tool needed was a crochet hook. Many crocheted articles were decorative doilies and mats to protect the furniture, or afghans to throw over the new settees. Victorian modesty was often preserved by covering the lid of the chamber pot with a crocheted silencer, so that it could be replaced in the night without anyone knowing it had been used. Tatting is a kind of lace-making involving looping and knotting cotton, linen or silk threads by means of a shuttle. It was entirely a decorative art, providing trim for household linens and clothing.

Straw press.

Handwork accessories
— tatting shuttles;
bodkins; thimbles;
wooden spool; pressed
straw sewing basket
with attached
pincushion (lid
missing).

SEWING

In the decade before Confederation ready-made clothing was available in stores in Ottawa, in larger towns, and even in village general stores. In the Ottawa *Citizen* of May 20, 1861, Fingland & Draper advertised themselves as "Importers of Dress Goods, Delaines, Prints, Cottons, Ribbons, Flowers, Feathers, Hats, Silks, Shawls, Mantles, Skirts, Hosiery, Gloves and Cloths." The Aylmer *Times* of August 22, 1866 stated that Stewart & Tierney of Arnprior had "Ready-Made clothing, Hats, Caps, Boots and Shoes all of which they offer cheap for cash or Country Produce." Dressmaking and tailoring establishments catered to the growing and prosperous middle class, but farm women were still providing many of the garments for their families.

Rural people often owned only two outfits each, one for everyday wear and one for special occasions. The arrival of the hand-operated sewing machine in the middle of the nineteenth century was a boon to those families who could afford one. Itinerant dressmakers and tailors sometimes stayed with a farm family long enough to provide a best outfit for each member, taking board as part of their pay. The materials used would be the housewife's own homespun cloth, with the possible addition of some cotton from the general store. If the family were affluent enough, the clothes would be cut out and made up. If not, they were cut out and left for the women of the family to finish. Silk was expensive and did not wear well, and was considered a luxury. Many a woman dreamed of owning one silk dress, but never saw her dream come true.

Clothes, once made, were passed down from older to younger children. Adult garments were taken apart and remade, and everything was mended until it was past any use except for the rag ball. Wooden darning eggs were used to stretch the worn-out part of the stocking or garment to ensure that the repair was woven smoothly. In the authors' collection is a flannel nightshirt containing a large patch, which has itself been mended. Basting threads were carefully removed and wound on spools to be used again. Before a garment was torn up for rags or cut into pieces for quilts, all buttons and trim were removed and saved to be re-used. Because of this thrift, and also because of the use of harsh soaps, everyday clothes of this period have not survived in large quantities, and much of the information about materials used has had to be based on studies of pieces found in old quilts.

Fashion-conscious women of this era wore hooped skirts which reached the ground. Crinolines would certainly have hampered rural women as they worked around the farm, both inside and out, and it is unlikely that they were worn around the home. In winter several underskirts gave a voluminous appearance to skirts, but this was more for warmth than adornment. However both hoops and the newly popular bustles were for sale in general stores, so they were probably worn for best. Caps of various kinds were worn by women in their homes, and sunbonnets protected their faces and necks when they worked outside in summer. Aprons were worn around the home to protect dresses and save laundering. Flannel nightshirts and nightdresses were worn by men and women, and they covered their heads with nightcaps to keep off the drafts in winter bedrooms. Children's clothing merely copied adult styles in miniature, adapted somewhat to children's active lives, and

Sewing machine.
– CANADA FARMER, 1870
NATIONAL MUSEUMS OF CANADA

the thrifty custom was to make the garment too large to start with so that the child could "grow into it." The ready-made articles most likely to be purchased by the farm family were men's felt hats and men's overcoats.

Most households consisted of extended families, and it was probably the grandmother or maiden aunt who made the rag dolls for little girls, and the doll clothes for the wooden dolls whittled by the men.

EMBROIDERY

Because of better lighting provided by kerosene lamps and the fact that stoves and kitchen gadgets were providing a little more leisure time, the rural women of the Valley were able to produce some needlework that was ornamental rather than essential. Little girls were still being taught the 12 basic embroidery stitches, but unfortunately the sampler was no longer commonly being used to teach stitches and alphabet and numerals. Very few samplers have been found that can be dated as having been made after 1850. Many, completed in the past, delightful in their originality, might still be hanging framed on parlour and bedroom walls.

Embroidery was worked on bedspreads and table cloths, clothing and handkerchiefs. Needlepoint chair coverings, pictures, cushions, fire screens and footstools began to crowd the new parlours. The growing number of periodicals and pattern books available to women brought about the gradual disappearance of the individually created designs of the past, and led to an upsurge in the use of mass-produced stamped designs. This was paralleled in the evolution of furniture, with the gradual disappearance of the individual craftsman and the rise in factory mass production.

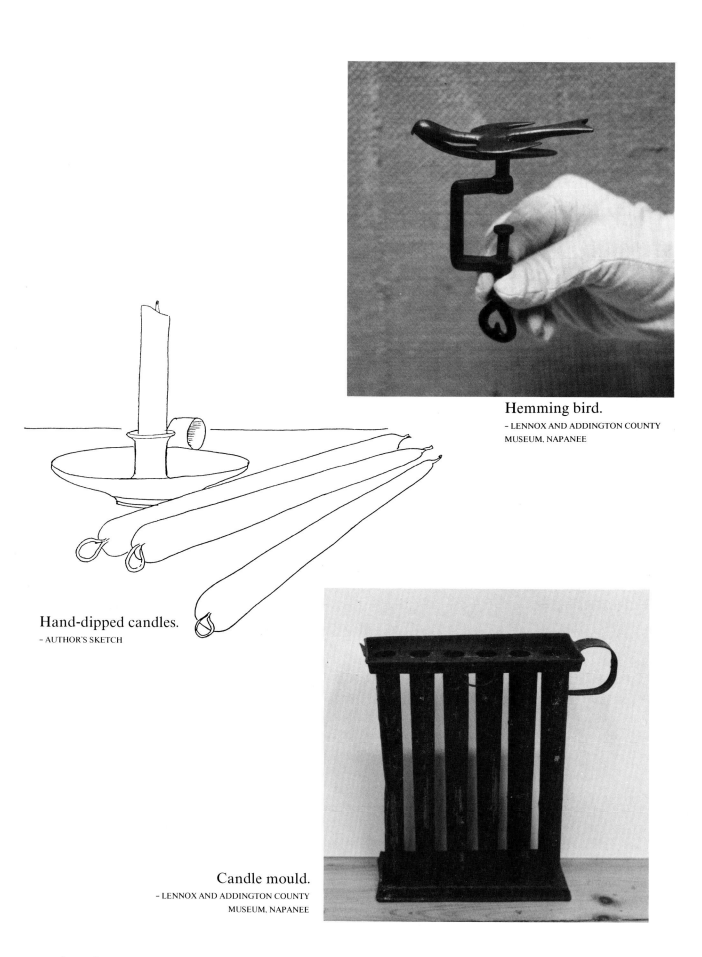

Hemming bird.
– LENNOX AND ADDINGTON COUNTY
MUSEUM, NAPANEE

Hand-dipped candles.
– AUTHOR'S SKETCH

Candle mould.
– LENNOX AND ADDINGTON COUNTY
MUSEUM, NAPANEE

Today we take needles and pins for granted, but in the past they were expensive, and were kept, when not in use, in needlecases or pin cushions. Cloth needlecases were home-made with decorated covers, and leaves usually made of flannel. Tubular cases could be purchased, made of wood or ivory or metal. Pin cushions were made of scraps of material in every imaginable shape and design, and could be found in every room in the house. Some of the small ones were filled with emery powder and were used to sharpen and clean pins and needles. Thread was bought on wooden spools, which were not discarded when empty, but saved to be used in spool furniture, as part of toys, or cut in half for drawer pulls. Embroidery scissors were made of steel and gilt or silver, and some had the owner's name incorporated into the handle design. Thimbles came in many materials and in all sizes, from those obviously made for little girls, to some large enough to have been used by men. Bodkins of brass or bone or steel were used for piercing and threading. The metal sewing or hemming bird was an ingenious device to provide an extra hand for the needlewoman. It could be clamped to a table or chair, and when the bird's tail was pressed the beak opened and held one end of a seam. This left both hands free to ply the needle and adjust the material. Some sewing birds even had a pin cushion attached for convenience.

LIGHTING

CANDLES

The most popular time to make candles was in the spring or fall, because they did not harden well in hot weather. Hard fat was saved and rendered by melting it in hot water, stirring it constantly with a wooden stick, and skimming off the melted fat as it rose to the surface. This was strained through a sieve or collander, the strainings saved for soap making, and the slab of clear tallow set aside to make candles by either dipping or molding. Cotton wicking was purchased from the store or from a pedlar.

Tallow dips were made by dipping the wicks many times in melted tallow, allowing each layer to cool and harden between dippings, until the candles reached the desired size. A common method of making a large number of dipped candles was to place two long poles parallel to each other across the backs of two chairs. Since double wicking gave a brighter flame, the wicking was cut twice the planned length of the candles, and draped across dowels or rods at regular intervals, about six to each dowel. These dowels were then placed at intervals across the parallel poles in a ladder-like arrangement. The tallow was remelted over hot water in a metal pot and the dowels, with wicks attached, were lifted off the poles, dipped in turn into the tallow, and replaced on the poles. By the time all had been dipped, the first were ready to be dipped again, and the process continued until all candles were large enough. At the outset the wicks had to be straightened after each dipping, but shortly the weight of the tallow made this unnecessary. By this process hundreds of candles could be made in a day.

Moulded candles could be made more quickly, were more uniform, and could be made when only a small amount of tallow was on hand. The moulds mostly were

Pierced tin lantern.

made of tin, and came in many sizes. Each wick was doubled and pushed through the hole at the end of the mould which would ultimately form the tip of the candles, and emerged at the top of the mould in the form of a loop. When all wicks were threaded, a stick was pushed through the loops to hold the wicks upright. The other end of the wick was then pulled taut and knotted. The melted tallow was carefully poured into each mould and allowed to cool. As it cooled the tallow shrank, so more was added to fill up the moulds. When the tallow had cooled, the knots at the bottom were cut, and the candles were carefully removed by lifting the sticks holding the loops. Sometimes the mould had to be dipped briefly in hot water to release the candles. Candles made by either method had to be stored in covered candle boxes because their animal fat content made them attractive to mice. Candles were put out as soon as possible after each use to make them last longer, and all ends and drippings were carefully saved to be rendered down to be used again.

Candles to be used outside and in the barn were placed in pierced tin and glass lanterns to protect them from the wind, and to make them safer for use among such combustible substances as hay.

If the charred wicks were trimmed at intervals candles burned more brightly, so metal snuffers were kept nearby. They had a pointed end to straighten the wick, a snipper of some kind, and a box arrangement to catch the sooty piece of wick, the snuff, after it was cut off. Snuffers were not used as extinguishers.

KEROSENE LAMPS

By the time of confederation, kerosene lamps were widely advertised for sale in both plain and fancy styles, for kitchen and parlour. Many rural families were happy to own just one lamp for the family to gather around in the kitchen, since it gave them the best lighting they had ever enjoyed. Candles continued to be used for a long time to light the way down to the cellar or up to the bedrooms, or for a trip to barn or outhouse. For some time the new lamps were regarded as dangerous, and were handled only by adults, and their use carefully supervised. The only tool associated exclusively with their use is the wick trimmer.

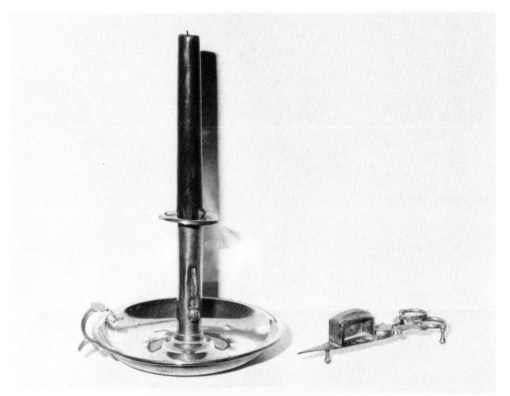

Candle stick and candle snuffer. - PRIVATE COLLECTION

Candle holder and
extinguisher.
- AUTHORS' COLLECTION

Splint and willow baskets. - AUTHORS' COLLECTION

Woodenware — clockwise l. to r.: clothes pegs; mortar and pestle; bottle stopper; line reel; spigot. - AUTHORS' COLLECTION

WOODENWARE

The old word "treen" meant any article, made from a tree, which had been produced for use, and not exclusively for decoration. The pioneer was, from the beginning, surrounded with an abundance of native woods which he transformed into useful objects, matching the differing qualities of the woods to their intended use. A farm boy, from about the age of eight, began to learn to work with a pocket knife and a piece of wood, learning the necessary skills he would need as the farmer he was expected to become. At first he made things for his own pleasure, such as willow whistles, tops or slingshots, but later would graduate to more useful objects.

As the nineteenth century advanced, factory-made wooden articles became available, but the farmer continued to use his skill and ingenuity to produce wooden articles for his home and farm at no cost. Many small domestic articles such as maple sugar spiles, wooden stoppers for crocks and bottles, bungs for barrels, clothes pins and so forth, were whittled by hand. The old gentlemen who passed their days in winter around the cracker barrel in the village store, or rocked in the summer sunshine on the porch, were often not "just whittlin'," but were producing useful objects.

One of the real nuisances the farm wife had to face was the presence of both rats and mice in home and dairy, and many clever types of hand-made wooden traps were produced in order to solve the problem. Some resulted in beheading the victim, others in crushing, drowning or hanging. Some trapped the rodent alive to be disposed of later. These traps are so complicated in some cases that they cause much bemusement among collectors of wooden artifacts. Factory-made traps were available as well.

Beautifully crafted domestic tools were favourite gifts from a young man to his intended bride. Most kitchen utensils were hung on the walls, so a matched set could be proudly displayed. In Ontario, the home craftsman depended on style and wood grain to make the finished article desirable. In Quebec this result was more often obtained by the use of carving. Since pine was the most suitable wood for carving, this mean it was often chosen for such article. The subjects reproduced were usually those encountered in daily life, such as animals, vegetables, grains and religious symbols.

When the weather did not permit outside work, tool handles were refitted or new ones made, as the family sat around the stove. This also would be the opportunity to pursue the lighter side of woodworking, the making of toys and sporting implements. Toys for girls were usually dolls and doll furniture and miniature domestic articles, while those for boys were toy-sized vehicles and animals. The handyman made baseball bats, sleds of all kinds, toboggans and showshoes. Skates could be fashioned from wood, with the skate blade made from an old file. Game boards were also made by hand, and the checkers used were, in some cases, dried cobs of corn sliced crosswise.

Almost anything in wood could be produced with the ubiquitous pocket knife and draw knife or spokeshave, with adzes and scorps for hollowing, and a piece of a broken mower blade for smoothing.

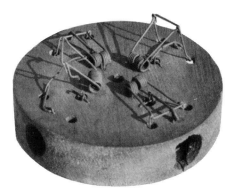

Factory-made wooden
mouse trap.

Assorted woodenware — clockwise l. to r.: pot
scraper; 2 vegetable mashers; wooden scoop; kitchen
hanger; fishing reel and float (pewter tablespoon for
size comparison).

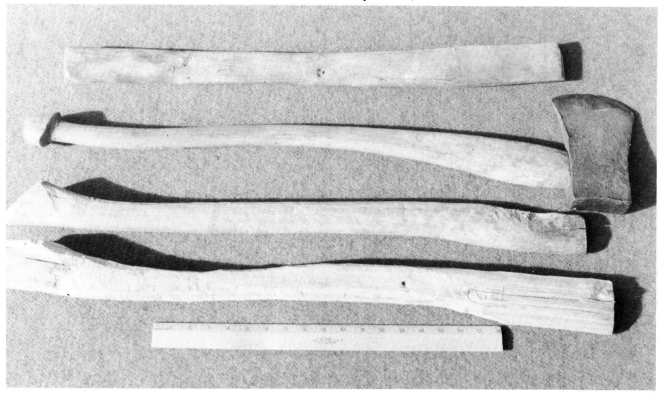

Handle-whittled axe handles.

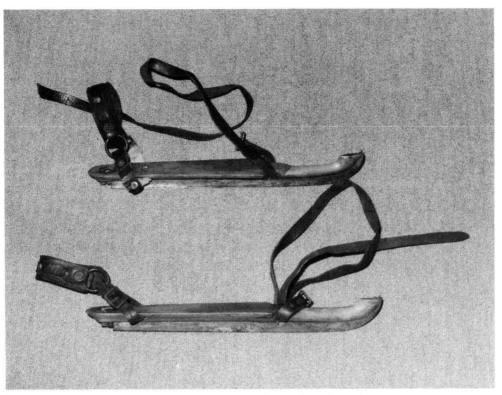

Factory-made skates of wood and steel. - AUTHORS' COLLECTION

Books and toys — bell; prayer book; 1860 history book; miniature sad iron; tole bubble pipe; miniature hatchet (large Canadian cent for size comparison).   - AUTHORS' COLLECTION

Privy door latch made of wood.

- LOG FARM MUSEUM, NEPEAN

Life in the Backwoods. – CANADA FARMER, 1864, NATIONAL MUSEUMS OF CANADA

CHAPTER 3
THE FARM

An OLD dictionary published in the mid-nineteenth century tells us that a farm is a tract of land cultivated by a single individual, whether as owner or tenant. This arid definition leaves out the intimate relationship between the farmer and his land — a relationship in which he develops an understanding of its potential and labours to bring it to fruition. An Ottawa Valley farm was not just a place to live and work, but a way of life for the farmer and his family.

The farm itself, as distinguished from the farm home, was considered the man's responsibility, even though the women and children were called upon to help as occasion required. The farmer's role was that of homebuilder, field husbandman, stockman, butcher, horticulturist and jack-of-all-farm-related-trades.

THE FIRST HOME

When the settler family arrived to face their raw bush property, they usually did so with limited tools, time, resources of manpower and materials, and often with a Canadian winter scant months ahead. Initially a suitable site had to be selected for their home and farmyard, taking into consideration drainage, freedom from large trees, and relationship to water supply and transportation routes. Next came the problem of clearing the area and cutting enough timber to construct a suitable all-weather shelter. This could be shanty-styled with a single slope to its roof, or a traditional two slope dwelling.

With his felling axe or brush hook, the settler "underbrushed" the area he was going to clear. This gave him room both to swing an axe, and later to draw away the logs and branches of the larger trees. The brush was piled in windrows and the standing timber then was felled. The large trees were limbed with an axe and cut into suitable transportable logs, keeping in mind the dimensions of the proposed dwelling. The cutting to length was often done with the two-man crosscut saw. The problem of the log shifting and the sawcut "binding" the saw was compensated for by driving sawyer's wedges into the cut behind the saw. These wedges were usually made with a hole through which a red cloth or some other suitable indicator could be threaded to reduce the likelihood of losing them in the debris of the forest floor. Eventually the time arrived when there was raw material enough for building the home, and a sufficient and convenient space on which to build. The immediate area to be built on was then cleared and levelled. This involved removing rocks, roots and stumps, reducing humps and filling hollows. The woodsman's axe was never used for the removal of roots because of the possibility of spoiling its keen edge on a boulder or a reef of bed rock. Mattocks or grub hoes, commercially manufactured or possibly blacksmith forged, were used to level the ground and to cut and dig out roots. Rocks were picked manually or pried out with bars. If the settler was fortunate

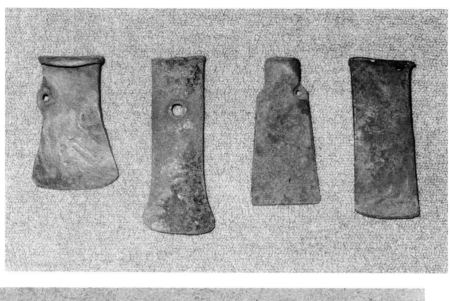

Sawyer's wedges.
- AUTHORS' COLLECTION

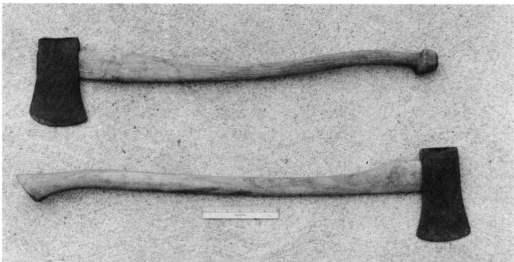

Felling axes.
- AUTHORS' COLLECTION

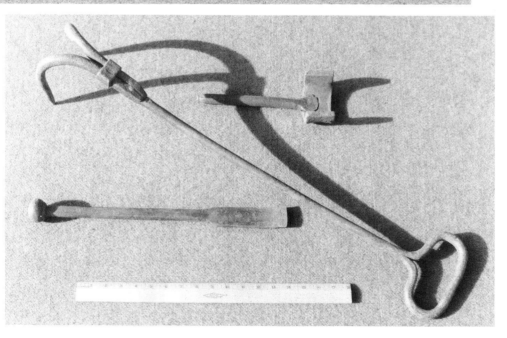

Bark spud; stone grubber; waggon wrench.
- AUTHORS' COLLECTION

Grub hoes.
- AUTHORS' COLLECTION

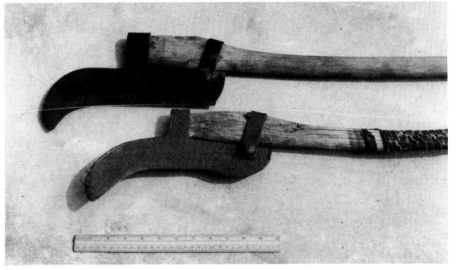

Brush hooks.
- AUTHORS' COLLECTION

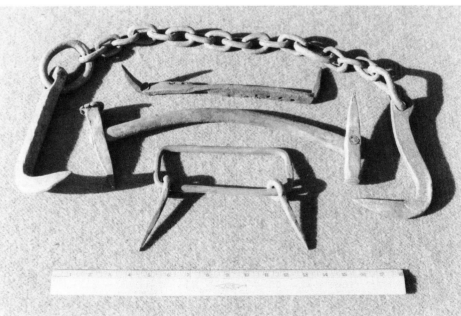

Log dogs — hand-
forged.
- AUTHORS' COLLECTION

enough to own a strong clawlike hook known locally as a stone grubber, he found that it not only saved the hands, but also gave a firm purchase on the rock to be moved. The dwelling was placed at the highest and dryest point, and set as level as possible.

Whether the settler's first home was a primitive shanty made from small logs in the round, or a cabin made from squared logs, depended on his financial resources, his skills, the availability of labour and the time of the year that it was started. Whatever the style, the log building was laid out on the bare ground and built up in the form of a box with, perhaps, arrangements for a door and fireplace. Other openings were sawn or chopped out if desired.

For a first-class snug dwelling, squared logs were used. They were formed by marking a log with chalk lines, notching the side of the log to these lines, and then hewing away the sections between the notches with a broad axe. This action was repeated until all four sides were squared, and a straight, smooth timber had been produced, usually 20 to 30 centimetres (8 to 12 inches) in cross section. The work of the skilled hewer of those days can still be seen in thousands of squared log buildings standing in the Valley today, some of which have withstood more than a century of summer rains and winter snows. Some workmen, when squaring and smoothing, used a carpenter's adze, a dangerous tool swung between the feet.

When squared logs were used for building, very effective corners could be made. There was the square-lapped joint made simply by the removal of half of the end of a log to engage a similarly notched log running at right angles to the first. The superior dovetail joint, however, was made with matching bevels and notches that fitted together, using the maximum amount of wood locked in both horizontal dimensions for a tight, dry joint. Usually this was the work of experienced "corner men." One can appreciate their skill when these beautiful joints are examined a century and more later. They were most effectively constructed by using a hand saw for the vertical cut and a hewing or carpenter's hatchet for chiselling out the longitudinal cut. The preliminary marking was probably done with a bevel, which is a squaring device which can be set to the necessary predetermined angle for an effective joint.

Plastering of chinks between the logs was an important part of the construction. The cracks were first partially closed with chips, sections of branches and moss. These fillers, then, could be cemented into place, and the holes stopped completely, by closing the spaces between the logs with a sand-lime mortar. It is likely though, that the first dwelling was caulked with a mortar made from the blue clay found nearly everywhere in the Valley. It was easy enough to construct a mortar-board and trowel from wood split out of timber. For later building the farmer probably provided himself with a carrying hod, which enabled him to carry his clay or mortar batch to any section and any level of the job. Some of these primitive plastering tools still turn up in old farm buildings throughout the Valley.

The roof of the home was dealt with in various ways. The roof rafters were often simply poles leading to a ridge pole. It was desirable that all unsquared poles or logs be debarked to minimize fungus rot and insect infestation. This was done with a barking spud — a type of long-handled chisel which served to pry the bark loose. These existed in many forms, depending on what the barking job was, and who had made the spud. A simple way to develop a waterproof roof was to split basswood or

Saddle-notch and scoop roof.
– UPPER CANADA VILLAGE, MORRISBURG

Dovetail joint — log
building.
– OTTAWA VALLEY FARM

Square-lapped joint
— log barn.
– OTTAWA VALLEY FARM

similar poles in half, lengthwise, using a steel wedge and a heavy wooden maul or beetle. The split poles were hollowed out with an axe, a gutter adze or similar tool, and then laid from ridge to eave in tile-like fashion — one pole to deflect the water, the next to conduct it to the eave.

This scoop roof was, at best, a makeshift approach, and was neither weather tight nor long-lasting. Sheets of elm bark were sometimes used in similar fashion with the same result. The better solution was the shingle. This was a tapered wafer of wood, 45 centimetres (18 inches) long and of varying widths, which had to be laid on a roof sheathing of sawn lumber.

In the transitional period of the mid 1800s manufacturing processes were taking place by methods varying from the primitive to the sophisticated. Roofing boards, for example, could be drawn by team and wagon from a sawmill where they had been cut by vertical gang or circular saws. On the other hand, pit saws for the hand-sawing of boards from a log were advertised in the Ottawa *Citizen* in 1865, and were being used, undoubtedly, where labour was plentiful and cash or kind were scarce. The pit saw or whip saw was a rip saw that was operated by two men, one on a platform and one below. The log was wedged on the platform using log dogs, if necessary, to hold the log in place, and boards were sawn from it by physical effort alone.

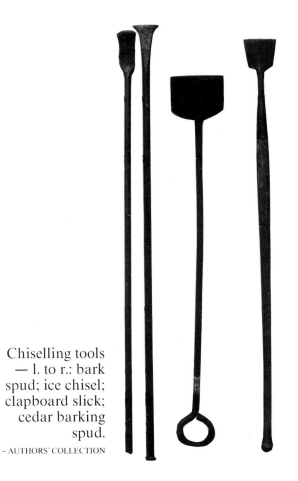

Chiselling tools — l. to r.: bark spud; ice chisel; clapboard slick; cedar barking spud.
- AUTHORS' COLLECTION

Adzes — l. to r.: gutter; carpenter's; shipwright's. - AUTHORS' COLLECTION

The variation in sophistication of production techniques applied also to shingles. By the 1860s shingle mills were producing a standard sawn shingle, but at the same time shake roofs were being applied, made from slices split from billets of cedar or pine logs with a froe (frow) and froe club. Shingles were also being produced in a similar fashion by splitting thinner slices from the billets and tapering them with a draw knife, using a shingler's bench as a vise to hold them in a working position.

The pioneer farmer used the same tools that he used to build his home to construct furniture and to manufacture equipment and implements with which to operate his farm. Augers were used to bore holes for legs and backs of chairs, and scorps (a type of one-handed gouging drawknife) for carving out butter bowls and other concave wooden objects. Basswood and pine were used where soft woods were required, but birch and maple were used characteristically for good hard timber. Unfortunately much of what was made was discarded when manufactured substitutes became available, too often burned or left in an outbuilding to decay. Thus countless wooden grain scoops and snow shovels, not to mention wooden household articles and small wooden tools, retreated progressively to the summer kitchen or the woodshed, and from there to the woodpile, barn, carriage shed and the dump pile or fire.

Two-man crosscut saw.
- LYALL CLARKE COLLECTION

Shingle froe (frow) in use.
- UPPER CANADA VILLAGE, MORRISBURG

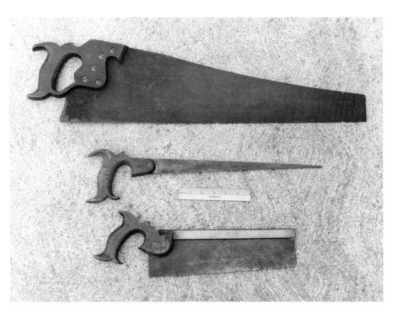

Three saws — bottom to top: back saw; keyhole saw; hand saw. - AUTHORS' COLLECTION

Four hatchets — l. to r.: hewing or carpenter's; shingling; lathing; claw.
- AUTHORS' COLLECTION

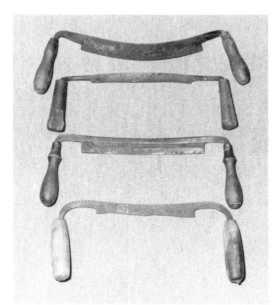

Draw knives.
- AUTHORS' COLLECTION

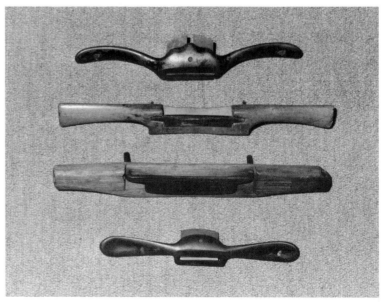

Spoke shaves.
- AUTHORS' COLLECTION

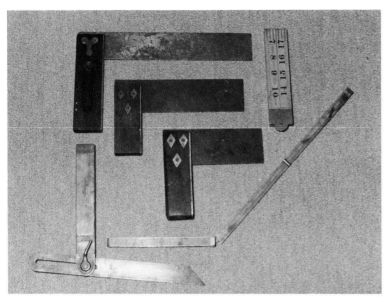

Bevel; try squares; rules
(folding). - AUTHORS' COLLECTION

Scorp. - AUTHORS' COLLECTION

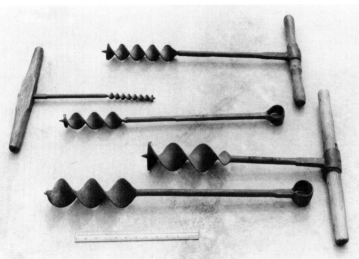

Screw augers (two-handed).
- AUTHORS' COLLECTION

Mortar tools — clockwise
l. to r.: carrying hod; mortar
board; wooden smoothing
trowel. - AUTHORS' COLLECTION

Wooden pump. – UPPER CANADA VILLAGE, MORRISBURG

THE WATER SUPPLY

As important as the building of a home, was the the provision of an assured water supply. Today's user of filtered, chlorinated water would pale at the thought of using a stream for the total needs of a farm family, which would include washing clothes, watering animals and providing water for cooking and drinking. Streams, however, provided many settlers with their water supply, and contributed, no doubt, to many pioneer deaths from typhoid fever, diphtheria and other water-borne diseases. Some families were fortunate enough to have year-round springs. Where no stream or spring served for a water supply, a well was a necessity.

Sometimes the water table was so high that the problem was to get a hole dug deeply enough for a suitable well before it was virtually full of water. The usual approach, however, was to begin with a hole wide enough to enable the digger to stand in it while excavating the first few metres with a shovel. Once the well became too deep to enable him to lift or throw the excavated soil to the surface, a "spoon" could be used. Basically, a spoon is a shovel blade mounted at a right angle to a long handle. It can be used for scraping soil from the bottom of a hole, and, because of its shelf-like effect, for lifting it to the surface. Once the well digger reached a depth where neither spoon nor shovel could conveniently remove the soil, he built a wooden crib to stop the walls from falling in and crushing him. Then, using a line and bucket and sometimes a windlass to haul up the soil to be removed, he would dig down until he struck water. Often water was not discovered until he had dug through a layer of hard pan or clay, and when the water stratum was reached the well could fill rapidly, making the provision of a ladder for escape a necessity.

Wells were usually lined (cribbed) with stone and/or wood, and were protected with a stone wall or wooden box at the surface. This kept dirt, rodents, snakes and frogs out of the water supply, and kept people and farm animals from falling in. Sometimes a roof was added to reduce the amount of surface water entering the well.

Water could be obtained by dipping from the well with a pail, or by the use of a pump. Lifting water with a pail normally involved a rope that was either hauled up hand-over-hand, by winding on a windlass, or by using a well sweep. The sweep did much to ease the task of drawing water. It worked on the principle of a counter-balanced lever. It consisted of a long pole balanced on an upright forked post, with the short heavy end of the pole weighted with rock, and the pail itself suspended from the long end. This end was pulled down to dip the pail in to the well, and the counterbalancing weight assisted in lifting out the full pail.

Pumps varied widely during this period. The wooden pump usually was constructed by local pump manufacturers. Occasionally a tool collector will be lucky enough to find at a farm auction one of the augers used in the manufacture of wooden pumps. This might possibly be because the pump maker was also a farmer, or because a farmer purchased the equipment when it fell into disuse, with the idea that it might come in handy around his farm some day.

At the same time that wooden pumps were being manufactured locally, every major foundry seemed to be advertising cast iron pumps in many models. There was also a chain pump which drew water to the surface with a system of little buckets on an endless chain, which emptied themselves into the well spout at the surface.

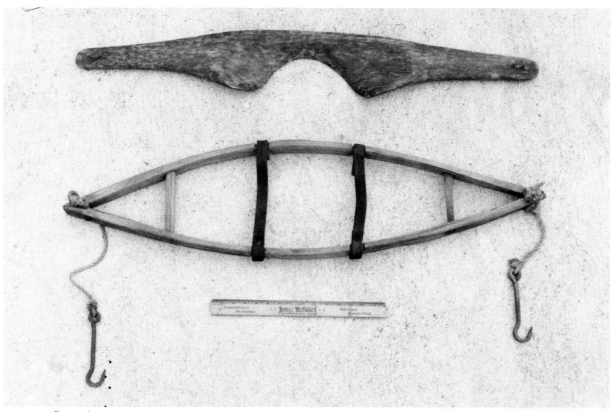

Carrying yokes. - AUTHORS' COLLECTION

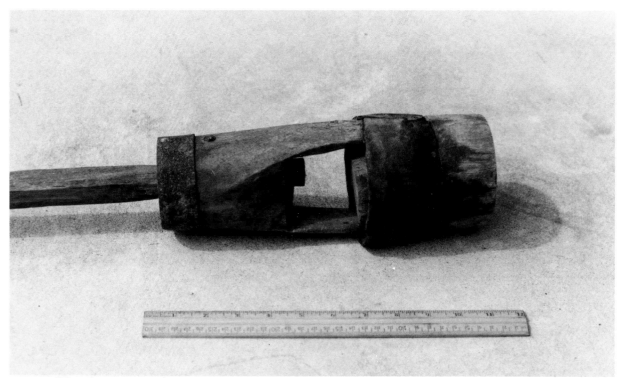

Wooden pump piston. - AUTHORS' COLLECTION

While the wooden pump was being replaced gradually by the more durable and reliable cast iron type, wooden pumps were still being made and used well into the twentieth century. Some, functional or otherwise, still grace old farmyards. The wooden parts, particularly the piston with its ingenious wood and leather construction, remain as interesting conversation pieces. While hand pumps have been replaced generally now by electric piston and centrifugal pumps, it is noteworthy that the nineteenth century models of cast iron pumps for yard and cistern continue to be made in substantially the same form in which they were manufactured over a hundred years ago.

To speed up and simplify the carrying of water to the house or outbuildings, a carrying yoke was used. This placed the combined weight of two pails of water on the yoke, which, in turn, put the pull directly onto the shoulders of the operator. The yoke was either carved from a single piece of pine or basswood, or was fabricated from wooden strips, with fabric or leather straps. The hooks to hold the buckets could be made of metal or suitably shaped pieces of a small branch. The yoke served its purpose well, but is looked back upon with little regret by those who remember carrying much water by this means.

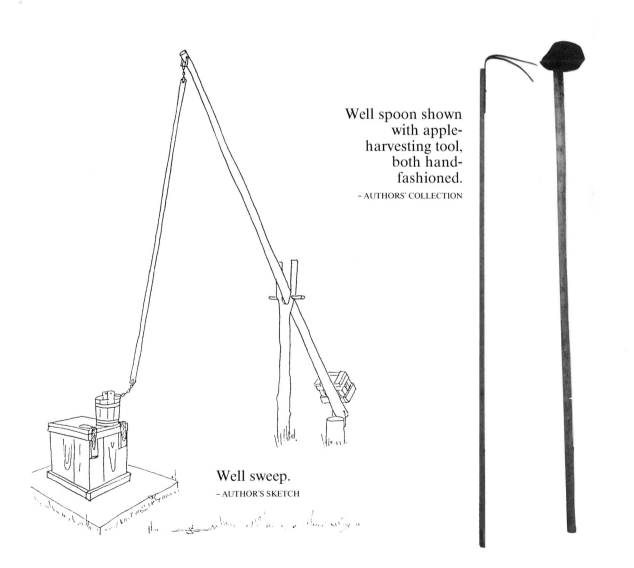

Well spoon shown
with apple-
harvesting tool,
both hand-
fashioned.
- AUTHORS' COLLECTION

Well sweep.
- AUTHOR'S SKETCH

FENCING

Once any significant clearing had been done and the fields were ready for their first crop, it was important that they be fenced. This was done primarily to ensure that roving livestock did not get into the crops. Fences were not only a physical necessity, but, in the event of someone else's cattle breaking into a farmer's crops, proper fencing was a legal requirement before a claim could be made against the owner of the offending animals. Fence viewers were appointed by the townships to see that fences were maintained to township standards. They travelled in pairs to settle disputes and make decisions about damages.

Some animals never understood that it was improper to breach a fence of legal dimensions, so if a cow broke through a proper fence on more than one occasion, it could be designated as a "breachy cow." Its owner was then required to pay damages for its depredations as they occurred. To prevent farm animals from breaching fences, various ingenious and widely varied devices known as "pokes" were suspended from their necks to enable the beast to graze comfortably, but at the same time make it impossible for it to get through or over a fence.

Cattle were sometimes contained by a fence improvised by drawing into line stumps left over from clearing the land. The first fences were usually made of whole poles requiring the use of hand tools. For rail fences the timber cleared from the fields was cut into rail lengths, about 3.5 to 4.5 metres (12 to 15 feet), using iron wedges and a heavy wooden maul or beetle. As the rail split lengthened, hardwood or iron gluts were used to hold the split open and expand it to the end. While cedar and ash were favourite woods for making good rail fences, any straight-grained wood could be used, and we hear of oak, elm, basswood and even black walnut fence rails.

The rail fence varied in form as well. The snake fence was easily constructed, but took up a good deal of extra space. A straight pole or rail fence was built with two upright posts driven in side by side, and rails or poles dropped into position between them. The use of posts, depending on the nature of the soil, sometimes presupposed the digging of post holes with a post hole auger or shovel, and possibly a spoon, for bringing debris out of the hole as it grew deeper.

Where posts had been dug or driven in, it was good practice in the spring, when the frost had gone out of the ground, to go down the line of posts with a post maul, giving each one a sharp blow to set it firm for another year.

The stones cleared from the fields were often piled at the base of the fence, forming an extra barrier, and giving support to the vertical stakes.

Log fences necessitated the moving and lifting of heavy logs, but did have the advantage of being formidable barriers, long lasting and not easily moved. The logs were laid overlapping one another at the ends, and resting on bunks or cross blocks which held them in place and separated them as well.

As time went on and farms became better groomed, some farmers replaced their old rail fences with a stronger, simpler design. Cedar posts 2 to 2½ metres long (7 to 8 feet) had five mortises about 5 by 13 centimetres (2½ by 5 inches) cut into them with a framing auger. Stout 3.5 metre (12 foot) rails were cut, the ends bevelled with an axe or a hewing hatchet, and inserted in the mortises. When the fence was

Snake fence.
- OTTAWA VALLEY FARM

Pole fence.
- OTTAWA VALLEY FARM

Log fence.
- OTTAWA VALLEY FARM

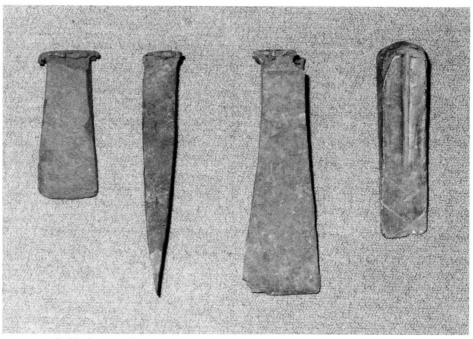

Splitting wedges. — AUTHORS' COLLECTION

Wooden mauls — sometimes known as beetles or commanders. - AUTHORS' COLLECTION

Post maul.
- H. RUPERT COLLECTION

Cow pokes. - AUTHORS' COLLECTION

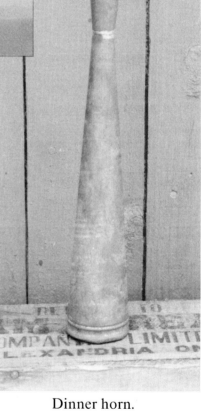

Dinner horn.
- LYALL CLARKE COLLECTION

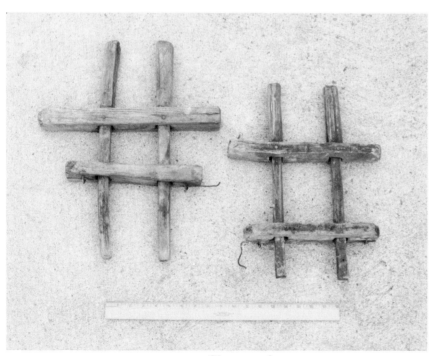

Sheep pokes. - AUTHORS' COLLECTION

complete one had virtually a solid unit as each post was locked into position with its rails, and vice versa.

Wire fencing was introduced in the 1860s, sometimes as a supplement to upgrade a rail fence, or as a fence in its own right. Wire had to be taut to be of any significant use, and its advent brought with it special tools such as fencing pliers, wire stretchers in many forms, and fencing staples. It was not until the advent of barbed wire and woven fences around the 1880s that wire fencing came into its own.

The subject of fencing should not be concluded without a comment on the use of bells. Cow bells (also used on horses), sheep bells and turkey bells were as important as fences for the control of animals when they were grazing free. Children, charged with bringing in the cows on their way home from school, located the animals by sound if they were not in sight. There were cast bells and factory-wrought bells, blacksmith-made bells, and crude home-made substitutes. It must have been a melodious age, with the use of animal bells, sleigh bells, field dinner bells, locomotive and steamboat bells, church and school bells to broadcast a message of some kind in a highly audible manner, and in ringing tones. The impact of the sound of the bell was not always that which was intended. On many farms the women summoned the men in from the fields for the mid-day meal by the use of dinner horns or bells. Horses learned the significance of the call, and upon hearing the familiar sound, sometimes refused further work, apparently to the point of rebellion that resulted in broken harnesses and equipment.

Animal bells: harness bells on straps; turkey, sheep and cow bells.
- LYALL CLARKE COLLECTION

Field dinner bell.
- OTTAWA VALLEY FARM

SOWING

The settler, having cleared a portion of his land, found himself with a field burdened with stumps, roots, rocks, hummocks and hollows that did not lend itself to soil preparation with oxen, harrows and plows. He was restricted to spreading the ashes produced by his land clearing, levelling by grubbing and raking, picking rocks, and then planting his seed on the unplowed surface and raking in the seed with a tree branch or similar drag.

Where wheat, which was a popular first crop, was sown, it was usually broadcast by hand from a seed bag slung over the shoulder, the traditional method used from biblical times. A wooden predecessor of the horse-drawn seed drill might also have been used. Suspended from the shoulders of the operator by a neck strap, it resembled a 3.5 metre (12 foot) length of eavestrough, with a perforated slide in the bottom, actuated by a wooden lever. By using this device the sower could spread a broad, uniform swath of seed as he progressed down the field. This broadcast approach was used also for oats, barley, rye, buckwheat and millet.

The main crops also included corn, potatoes, pumpkins, peas, beans and turnips, which had to be sown more tediously. Where the land would permit its use, home-made markers established the direction and distance of separation of the row plantings.

Potatoes, corn and pumpkins could be planted in evenly-spaced shallow hollows or "hills," which were mounded by scraping the surrounding earth over them with a hoe. Potatoes were cut into chunks, each including at least one sprouting "eye." The number of pieces planted in each hill depended upon the preferences of the individual farmer.

Corn could also be sown in drills, which were long furrows excavated with a hoe, and closed after planting. Pumpkins and watermelons were often planted at intervals as a companion crop. Field peas for food and forage, beans for harvesting as dry beans, turnips and mangolds for animal feed, were all sown in drills.

Corn planting by hand was mechanized gradually with hand-operated corn planters, which enabled the sower to insert seed precisely where required, without stooping. By the late 1860s wheeled seed planters had been developed, which opened the furrow, deposited the seed in a predetermined quantity, and closed the furrow again as the operator pushed the implement along a marked course.

The concept of seeding must include the planting of fruit trees such as the apple. By the middle of the nineteenth century the farmer was heir to a large amount of technical competence that had been developed in fruit growing, both with respect to the fruits themselves, and to the equipment that was used. Budding knives, pruning knives and pruning saws became part of the equipment of the orchardist. It is more than likely, though, that the jack knife and handsaw served the purpose on many farms.

SUMMER CARE OF CROPS

The summer care of the crops was mainly one of weeding, cultivation, watering the vegetables and nursery stock, and dealing with plant pests and diseases.

The control of insects was somewhat more selective that today's universal plant

Hand-operated corn planter.
- AUTHORS' COLLECTION

Plant duster.
- AUTHORS' COLLECTION

sprays. Potato bugs were picked by hand, dropped into a container and disposed of by burning. Some insects were shaken or brushed from plants onto cloth spread beneath the plant and burned. Slugs were controlled by quicklime dusting, sulphur was used for red spider, and hellebore dusted onto plants to get rid of currant saw flies.

Plant dusting was accomplished by such simple processes as sifting the powder onto the plant through coarse cloth material tied on the end of a tin can. In the authors' collection is a tinsmith-made duster with a row of holes to allow the dust to fall through, and a hollow tin handle, obviously meant to be extended by a pole. When purchased it still held a dusting of what seemed to be flowers of sulphur and lime.

Wheeled seed drill. - BLOCKHOUSE MUSEUM, MERRICKVILLE

HARVEST

The principal cereal crops had to be harvested manually until fields were cleared sufficiently for the use of machinery. This was done with a scythe, grain cradle or sickle. Both the scythe and grain cradle could be used in an upright position, with rhythmic, telling strokes, but there were spots where a sickle could be more easily used around stumps and roots. This sickle, common in both Quebec and Ontario, was a heavier, sturdier tool than the reaping hook of the Atlantic Provinces or the New England States. The scythe and grain cradle were operated with the same swinging motion, but the cradle enabled the operator to deposit a bundle of grain at the end of each stroke, whereas rakers were required to follow the sickle or scythe before the bundles could be collected, tied into snug sheaves with a twist of grain straw, and stooked for drying. The men usually did the cutting while the women gathered and tied the sheaves with the straw "bands."

Once dry, the crop was forked onto the wagon and hauled to the barn, where it might be threshed immediately or stored inside or outside in a carefully built stack, until a more convenient time for threshing.

Hand threshing was done on the threshing floor, which was usually a tight double floor to prevent the loss of grain. It stood between the front and back doors of the barn, thus providing, hopefully, a cross wind for blowing away the dust and chaff. In hand threshing the cut grain sheaves were tossed onto the threshing floor and beaten with a flail.

Grain cradle. - AUTHORS' COLLECTION

Two scythes — a longer bladed scythe for hay or grain, shorter for heavy weeds or light brush.
- AUTHORS' COLLECTION

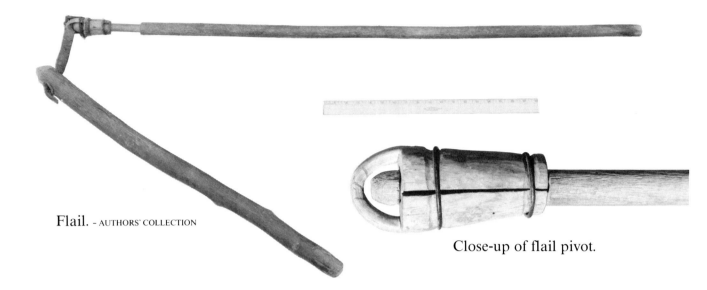

Flail. - AUTHORS' COLLECTION

Close-up of flail pivot.

Flails depended for their action on a free-swinging wooden arm suspended from a wooden handle by a leather thong, or by a combination of a skilfully whittled wooden ball and socket joint from which the arm was suspended — again by a thong. The size and weight of the flail arm varied, presumably with the size or wishes of the owner. Some are so heavy that a day's activity with a flail must have been a gruelling experience. As the grain was beaten loose from the straw, the straw was tossed aside with a fork, and from time to time the residue that lay on the floor was shovelled into a winnowing basket or tray. These were tossed or shaken so that the grain fell to the floor and the lighter, coarser seed hulls, pieces of broken straw and grain heads, dust and fine weed seeds, hopefully, were blown outside by the cross draft. The remaining straw was forked into the mow for animal feed and bedding.

By the 1860s the winnowing process had been taken over by the fanning mill wherever money was available to buy such equipment. This apparatus, turned either by hand or horse power, could rapidly and successfully rid the grain of chaff, dirt and weed seeds with its fan-type blower and series of oscillating screens.

Corn was the single exception to the ordinary processes for cereal harvesting. Corn harvesting, by hand, was done with a type of machete called a corn knife, a corn-cutter which looked like a long-handled straight-bladed sickle, or corn hoe, which latter was, apparently, the most effective and comfortable to use.

Once cut, the corn was husked with one of a variety of hand-held husking pegs and stored to dry in corn cribs until shelled. Hand-operated mechanical shellers were available for this work.

Much of the grain, including corn, was bagged for handling. As the farm and crops and barns grew larger, the filling and handling of bags was simplified with equipment such as grain scoops, grain measures, and two-wheeled push trucks.

Corn-harvesting tools, top to bottom: corn hook; corn hoe; corn knife; hand-made corn chopper.
- AUTHORS' COLLECTION

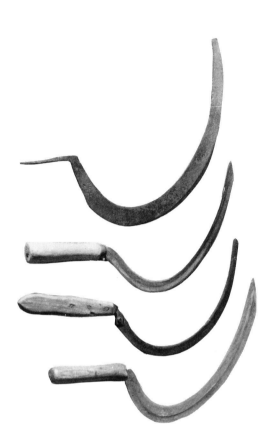

Assortment of sickles.
- AUTHORS' COLLECTION

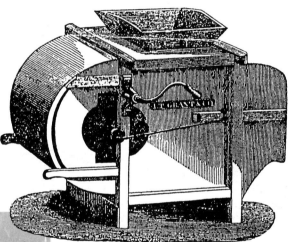

Fanning mill.
- NATIONAL MUSEUMS OF CANADA

Corn sheller.
- AUTHORS' COLLECTION

Bushel grain measure next to sap bucket
for size comparison. - AUTHORS' COLLECTION

Grain scoops
— note
wooden D
handles
characteristic
of period.
- AUTHORS'
COLLECTION

Two-wheeled push truck.
- AUTHORS' COLLECTION

HAY

Hay was not grown as a cultivated crop on the early farms because of the difficulty of harvesting it, and the worth of hay as a fodder or cash crop compared to that of other crops. When hay was harvested, it was often from marshy areas known as beaver meadows. The hay crop would be heavy in such locations, but would have to be carried out on poles to a waiting hay rack, as the ground would usually be too wet to support the weight of a team and wagon. It would be necessary to cut the hay with a scythe or cradle as it was unlikely that a mower could operate there either. After drying in the field, during which time it was turned with hay forks, it was raked into small coils, using either the regular wooden farm grass rake, or the big wooden bull rake, which handled the heavy marsh grass and bundled it into large masses. These masses felted themselves into a cohesive bundle that enabled two men to pass poles through a bundle and carry it out. The hay was then stored in a stack near the barn, or, preferably, in the barn loft itself.

When the farmer was ready to use his hay, the easiest way to get it out of a densely packed stack was with a razor-sharp hay knife. This cut out a section without disturbing the rest of the hay, and made forking it out a simpler task.

Hay knives — note top knife fashioned from a broken crosscut saw.

Bull rake. - BLOCKHOUSE MUSEUM, MERRICKVILLE

Wooden hay fork.
- BLOCKHOUSE MUSEUM, MERRICKVILLE

Wooden grass
rake.
- AUTHORS' COLLECTION

Two metal hay forks — one hand-
forged and one factory-made.
- AUTHORS' COLLECTION

Wooden barley fork.
- AUTHORS' COLLECTION

ROOT CROPS

The last of the annual crops to be brought in from the field were the potatoes and turnips. The farm family had undoubtedly been eating new potatoes since July, but once the vines withered, the crop was mature and ready to be dug. If possible potatoes were harvested on a warm dry day to set the skins and allow any residual soil to dry and fall away before they were bagged for storage.

Many potatoes came up with the roots when the withered tops were pulled. The remainder were carefully unearthed with a garden fork or a potato hook. The latter looked like a garden fork that had been bent into a long-tined rake. Potatoes were then stored in the house cellar, root cellar or temporary field storage pits or "clamps."

Depending on the success of the crop and the nature of the soil, turnips could be easy or difficult to harvest. Large turnips in heavy soil needed the firm assistance of a garden fork or shovel to free them. They were topped with a heavy knife, allowed to dry as potatoes were, and stored in a field pit or root house.

Loading turnips. - ONTARIO MINISTRY OF AGRICULTURE AND FOOD

The turnip is a desirable form of animal as well as human food, and in the past was used more for fodder than it is today. It is not edible for livestock in its hard round form, however, and so has to be cut into suitable hunks or slices. Anyone who has sliced a single small turnip for table use, will realize the difficulty of providing sufficient quantities of the sliced vegetable for even a single cow. This need was met by a variety of hand-operated mechanical slicers. In the authors' collection is an interesting machine made out of hardwood with a guillotine knife operated by a wooden lever, and fed by a gravity feed. The blade is fashioned with knives extending from its inner face to slice and cut the slices into sections in the same operating stroke. Other root slicers worked on the basis of rotating blades like a large meat slicer.

The same slicing process was used with the mangolds or mangel-wurzels, a large coarse yellow-orange beet, which was also excellent cattle food.

Wooden root cutter, home-made.
- AUTHORS' COLLECTION

Two factory-made root cutters.
- CANADA FARMER, 1866
NATIONAL MUSEUMS OF CANADA

BEEKEEPING

Honey bees were not indigenous to North America, and various strains were imported from Europe and Asia Minor to the United States. It is recorded that they were brought into Canada as early as 1792.

"Bee-lining" was practised to discover bee colonies that had established themselves in the wild. This consisted of capturing a honey bee and putting it in the darkened side of a bee-hunting box for a couple of days. Then it was allowed into the windowed section containing dilute honey, and kept there for 48 hours longer. After that, the bee was released, the object being to follow it back to its hive, cut down the tree which contained it, cut out the hive and bring it back to the farm.

By the 1860s there were several patented hives on the market, similar in appearance to those of today. Hives were managed with the object of keeping the bees well supplied with food and space, and providing a proper temperature for health and high honey production.

The tools used were similar in design to those used today, with decapping knives, bee smokers and simple extractors for removing honey from the comb.

Bees were important for orchardists and seed growers and, in addition to supplying another native sweetening besides maple sugar, served to pollinate the fruit trees at blossom time. The wax produced by the honey bees was used for many purposes. It can still be found in old sewing boxes as a block through which linen thread was pulled to wax it. If added to the tallow it produced harder candles. It was used for sealing jars and bottles, and, in combination with other oils and waxes, was made into polishes.

Beehive.
- CANADA FARMER, 1866
NATIONAL MUSEUMS OF CANADA

Bee Smoker.
- AUTHORS' COLLECTION

FARM ANIMALS

Raising, caring for, and ultimately disposing of the large farm animals was considered to be the work of the men of the farm family. However, as in all farm work, there was occasional or consistent sharing of responsibilities, depending upon circumstances. Cows had to be milked twice a day, and while this was apparently done by the women on many farms, on others the older boys or men might assume responsibility.

The draught animals, oxen and horses, were virtually daily companions of the farmer, and required daily wiping, brushing and combing. This grooming was done sometimes with a cloth, a horse brush and a curry comb. However a firm handful of hay and a corncob often provided an acceptable substitute.

Sheep were sheared with a simple hand shear. To do this effectively and painlessly for the sheep required a combination of strength and skill.

Apart from hauling and the provision of dairy products and wool, the large animal was important for meat production as well. The farmer was usually his own butcher, although neighbours sometimes shared the slaughtering jobs on one another's farms in turn.

Every old farm seems to have one or more gambrel sticks tucked away in a corner or lying on a shelf. These were used to slide into a slit cut between the hamstring tendon and the leg-bone of the hind legs of slaughtered hogs, enabling the carcass to be strung up by a pulley from a pole, tripod or a beam to be dressed. In the hog slaughter the farmer used a scalding kettle and hog scrapers to rid the carcass of its bristles. It was hauled in and out of the scalding kettle with a hand-fashioned hog hook and cut up with a massive cleaver, a meat saw and heavy butcher's knives, the latter sometimes fashioned from old files.

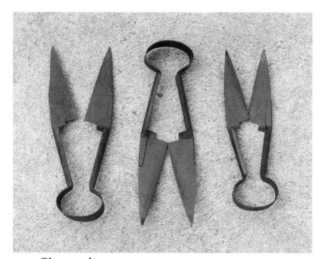

Sheep shears. - AUTHORS' COLLECTION

Killing and Scalding Hogs.

- CANADA FARMER, 1866, NATIONAL MUSEUMS OF CANADA

Slaughtering a beef animal involved removing the hide in the process, and was a heavier but similar operation. Sheep too were skinned, not scalded. The hides in both cases were usually tanned by a local tanner.

The gross cutting, hanging and packing of the meat was done by the men, who then turned the remaining meat preparation over to the women, to be done inside. When the meat was ready for smoking, however, the process was again the responsibility of the men. Smoke houses varied considerably from farm to farm, but they were essentially roofed sheds built with rough lumber, with the boards separated by a finger's breadth from one another to allow the smoke to escape slowly. The smoke house was fitted out with hooks for hanging fish, bacon, sausage, hams or whatever was to be smoked. The smudge fire of maple, birch, hickory or apple was made in a container such as an old "cooler," so that there would be no draft and resultant quick flame. It would smoulder away and be renewed when it went out.

Many, if not most, farmers were either out of reach of a qualified veterinarian, or so far away that valuable time would be lost in reaching him. Farmers therefore had to cope with all the problems of calving, lambing and littering among their stock. They had to deal with tooth irregularities and abscesses, with foreign bodies in the eye or with accidental cuts and with diseases, from the scours to colic. The farm papers of the day were well provided with advertisements for self-help books for the stockman. Some of the treatments proposed sound murderous today. Many patent medicines were universal panaceas for man or beast. The farmers, however, some more effectively than others no doubt, poulticed and anointed their animals, often to good effect. The experienced stockman might end up with a small outfit of instruments that could include a spring "Bull Dog" to snap into the nose of cattle to hold them, and a twist or "twitch" to maintain control of horses, a shoeing or

Gambrel sticks. - AUTHORS' COLLECTION

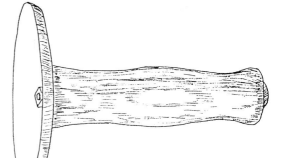

Hog scraper: the scraper is, essentially, a sturdy steep-walled metal saucer bolted to a wooden handle. Once the hog carcass has been scalded and the bristles thus loosened, the scraper is then used to remove the bristles from the skin. - AUTHOR'S SKETCH

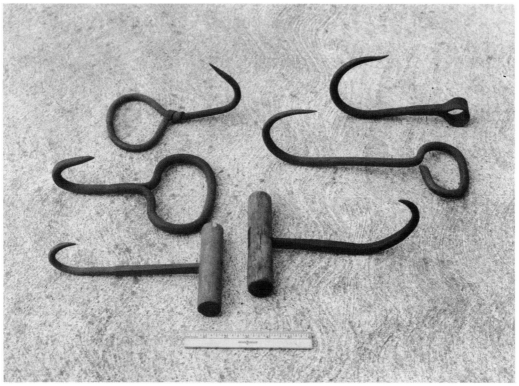

Hog hooks, hand-forged. - AUTHORS' COLLECTION

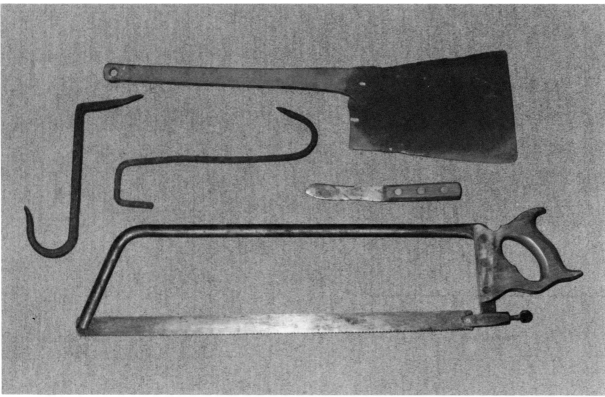

Butchering tools — top to bottom: cleaver; hand-forged meat hooks; butcher knife; meat saw. - AUTHORS' COLLECTION

Heating water for hog butchering.
- UPPER CANADA VILLAGE, MORRISBURG

Hog butchering.
- UPPER CANADA VILLAGE, MORRISBURG

Smoke house.
- UPPER CANADA VILLAGE, MORRISBURG

farrier's knife, a clinical thermometer, a firing iron for cauterizing, a pair of spring forceps, clamps for castration, a few surgical needles with some silk thread and a bit of cat gut (stored in alcohol to keep it clean and pliable), a scalpel (though a sharp jack knife might have to do), a syringe for cleaning out wounds, and a rasp for filing teeth. A favourite tool of the day was the fleam, a special blade used for bleeding animals.

Some farmers became well known in their localities for their demonstrated skill in treating animals, and were in great demand by their neighbours. Without detracting from the stockman's reputation, it speaks well for the innate robustness of some animals that they recovered not only from their affliction, but from the treatment as well.

CIDER

When a farmer had surplus apples he often made cider for the use of the family. The instructions in the *Canadian Farmer*, a farm periodical of the day, suggested that the fruit be harvested when fairly ripe and be picked over to remove any wormy or decayed specimens. The fruit was then to be piled in small heaps to "sweat" for a few days, but not to be allowed to get overripe. At that point the apples were ready to be pulped in a cider mill and put into a cider press.

After pressing, the sweet cider was then put into clean casks with a few centimetres of head space, and allowed to ferment. A week later it was "racked" into a fresh cask. This was repeated after 10 days, and, finally, after a further 15 days. After the last racking the cask was filled full, bunged tight, and stored in a cold, frost-proof cellar.

Cider mill and press.
– CANADA FARMER, 1868
NATIONAL MUSEUMS OF CANADA

H. Sells' Patent of 1866.

THE OUTBUILDINGS

The characteristic Ottawa Valley farm of the Confederation era often presents a harmony of purpose, colour and shapes in the complex of buildings that have risen to meet the needs or ambitions of the farmer and his family. Smoke-houses and hen houses, pig pens and sheep byres, horse stables and cow barns, pump houses, woodsheds, milk houses, duck pens, carriage sheds, storage sheds and work shops have been built as needed, at different times and of different materials. No matter what state the farm is in today, at some point in time each of these buildings was required to keep the whole operation effective.

Dominating the assembly of outbuildings is the large, high-lofted barn that is still the pride of the Ottawa Valley farm scene. It is with a pang of regret that one sees the rapidly declining condition of many of these centenarians today. They can never be replaced — partly because the time has passed when neighbours gathered at a "bee" and provided free labour to erect a barn, and partly because the farmer no longer has access to low cost timber resources or a supply of people skilled enough to transform it readily into a finished building.

The frame barn was made with post and beam construction as compared to the box-like log barn. The individual members of the frame were timbers, generally 20 to 30 centimetres (8 to 12 inches) square, notched and hewn from oak, ash or other hardwood logs. The whole framework was carefully measured and cut before being assembled. This involved the careful use of rules and squares, and a high degree of precision cutting, drilling and chiselling in the preparation of the mortise and tenon joints that held the barn together.

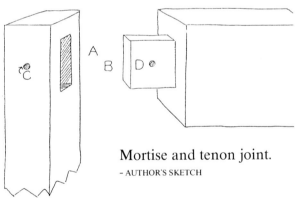

Mortise and tenon joint.
- AUTHOR'S SKETCH

Mortises were cut using a two-handed auger or its successor, the boring machine. For a 5 by 15 centimetre mortise, for example, three 5 centimetre (2 inch) holes were drilled side by side in a line, and the spare wood chiselled out with a mortising or corner chisel and mallet. The tenon was cut to size with a handsaw and a hewing or carpenter's hatchet. The timbers were then driven into position using a heavy wooden mallet or beetle, and the joint secured with a hardwood "trunnel" or "tree nail" driven into a hole that had been bored through the mortise and the tenon.

The remainder of the outbuildings reflected, in their form and appearance, the time of their building, the building materials available, the prosperity and effective husbandry of the farmer, and the original purpose to which they had been put. Thus today on the same farm you may see a dozen outbuildings built variously from log or board and batten, clapboard, stone or cement.

Boring machine. - AUTHORS' COLLECTION

Wooden mallets — (left) 2 oak,
(right) 2 burled walnut.
- AUTHORS' COLLECTION

Trunnel for holding tenon in
mortise. - AUTHORS' BARN

Wooden pulleys. - AUTHORS' COLLECTION

Buggy jack. - AUTHORS' COLLECTION

Waggon jack. - AUTHORS' COLLECTION

123

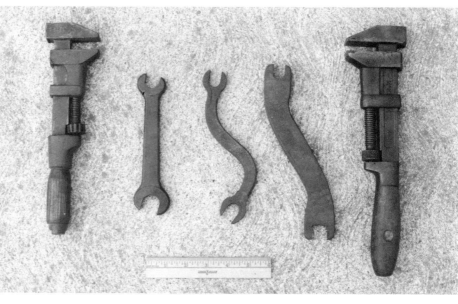

Screw wrenches and
spanners.
- AUTHORS' COLLECTION

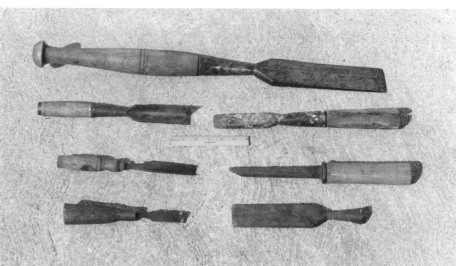

Chisels.
- AUTHORS' COLLECTION

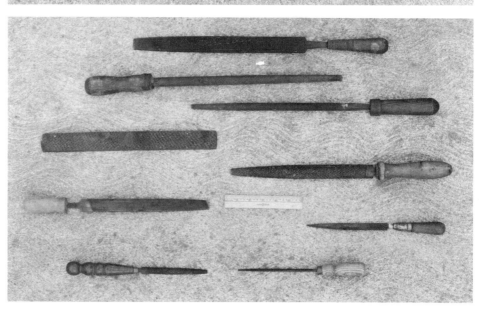

Rasps and files.
- AUTHORS' COLLECTION

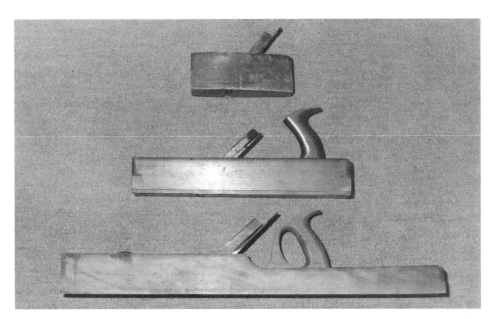

Planes — smoothing,
jack and trying.

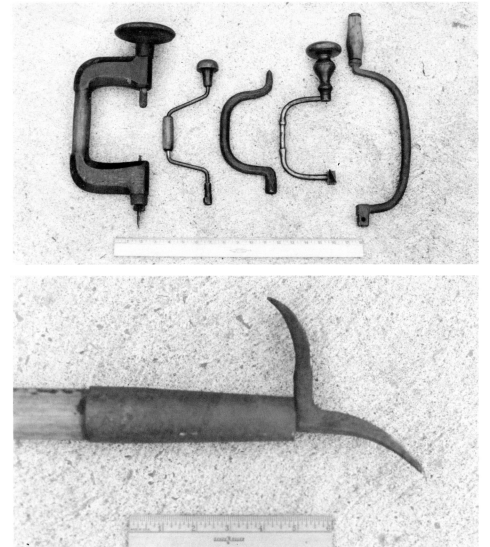

Boring braces.

Pike pole "pike".

CONSTRUCTION, REPAIR AND MAINTENANCE

The process of construction must have seemed a never-ending task on a developing farm in a period of rapid agricultural change — change in crop demands, change in technology and change in agricultural economics.

An inevitable consequence of ownership of buildings and equipment is the problem of repair and maintenance. The installation of a scoop roof meant that five or six years later the farmer was busy taking off the old roof, putting sheathing across his rafters, and installing shingles, using, in all likelihood, the popular shingler's hatchet. This enabled him to split shingles to the right size, nail them on, and, if a nail was bent, to pry it loose with the notch provided in the blade.

The axles of wagons and carriages had to be greased and repairs effected. If the horses became excited and broke an oak wagon tongue, spanners or screw wrenches were used to unscrew the nuts on the broken tongue and the bolts were driven out with a drift. A new piece of oak had to be sawn to length and shaped and smoothed with a draw knife, rasps or a plane, bored with a brace and bit or two-handed auger to provide new bolt holes, and the new tongue bolted into place.

Grease, be it tallow, castor oil or mineral greases (for all had their own lubricating role), was not held in wheel bearings as effectively as it is in today's automobile, but was just as essential to the reduction of wear and promotion of ease of performance. Wagons and carriages had to be jacked up using home or factory-made wagon or buggy jacks, the wheels removed with special wagon or buggy wrenches, the wheel and axle cleaned and regreased, and each wheel reinstated with just the right amount of "play" to allow it to roll freely.

The net result of this constant requirement of repair and maintenance was the setting up of workshop space for both a farm blacksmithing operation, however simple, and a wood-working area, for virtually everything the farmer used was either made primarily of wood, or had a wooden component.

THE FARM WORKSHOPS

Blacksmithing

The farm smithy attended to many simpler wants which did not justify going to the closest blacksmith shop, which would have meant loss of time on a busy day, as well as a bill to pay. The farmer did not need to be a professional blacksmith to carry out the fundamental practices of welding, drawing out (lengthening), upsetting (shortening and thickening) and tempering (developing appropriate hardness). Once he had learned these he could weld chains, make hooks, rings and clevises and sharpen harrows, picks and mattocks. In a period when "use up and make do" was a watchword, he could cut down old scythe blades to make vegetable choppers, forge old files into farrier's tools and return grain scoops and shovels to use by rivetting sections of old metal pails over the holes worn in them. He repaired tin and copper kettles, teapots, pails and boilers with a soldering iron and a bit of solder, and did minor horseshoeing tasks. Because of the supporting slings that were required to hold an ox up while shoeing was being done, it is likely that oxen were taken to the blacksmith to be shod.

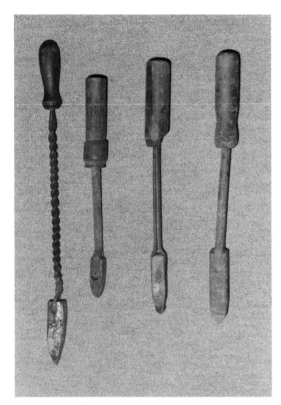

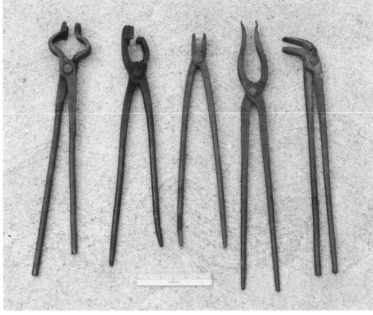

Blacksmithing tools: pincers.
- AUTHORS' COLLECTION

Soldering irons.
- AUTHORS' COLLECTION

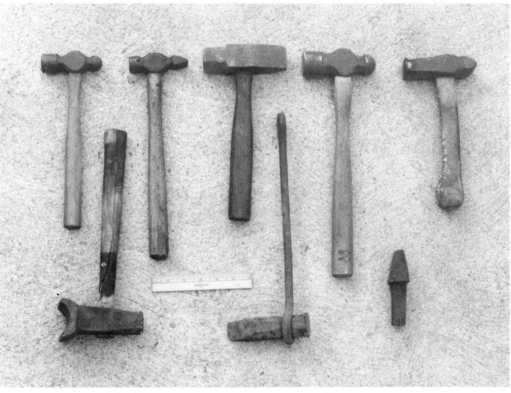

Blacksmithing tools: hammers and cutters. - AUTHORS' COLLECTION

Stockman's tools — clockwise from top: farrier's tool box; horse tooth rasp; farrier's pincers; clinch cutter for straightening or cutting horseshoe nails; cattle leader; jacknife; farrier's knife; hoof parer; farrier's nippers; horse hoof rasp; curry comb.
- AUTHORS' COLLECTION

Butteris.
- AUTHORS' COLLECTION

Horseshoes could have surprising uses. Here two have been forged into a hinge. - AUTHORS' COLLECTION

Farrier's hoof rest for supporting hoof during shoeing operations.
- AUTHORS' COLLECTION

Every smithy required a forge and bellows and an anvil. The other essentials were hammers, a workbench and a vice, plus a small collection of tongs, chisels, pincers and hardies.

To make his horseshoeing tasks simpler, the farmer could add a pair of nail clippers to pull worn nails out of the hoof, hoof parers, a horse rasp for levelling the hoof, a clinch cutter for cutting nails before removing the shoe, clinching blocks to use in tightening the shoe against the hoof, and a farrier's knife. Add to this collection a few punches and drifts, a drill stock and bits, a nail header or so for making his own nails, and you have a list of most of the common tools that would have been found in a farm smithy.

One of the less commonly found hoof-paring tools is the butteris. It has a chisel-edged lower end with an extended handle, ending in a pad that fits into the shoer's shoulder. The operator presses his shoulder into the pad to develop the necessary force to cut the hoof. The unusual name and method of employment, added to its comparative rarity, have made it a tool collector's delight.

Woodworking

Farms seldom had enough ready space for all the things the farmer had to do. It was essential, however, that he set aside a place in which to do simple construction and repair. It had to be a safe place out of the rain to store his tools and supplies, a spot near a window if possible, with room for a workbench. Such an area served as his woodworking shop.

The *Canada Farmer*, in an article of 1869 entitled the "Family Tool Chest," said: "There should be an axe, a hatchet, a large wood saw — also with a buck or stand if wood is burned, a claw hammer, a mallet. Two gimlets of different sizes, two screwdrivers, a chisel, a small plane, one or two jack knives, a pair of large scissors or shears, a carpet fork or stretcher, an assortment of nails from large spikes down to small tacks, not forgetting brass-headed nails; screws of various kinds as well as hooks."

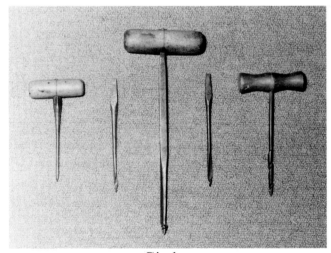

Gimlets. - AUTHORS' COLLECTION

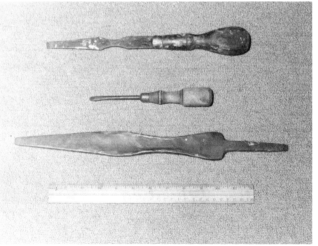

Screwdrivers — bottom one (handle missing) made from an old file.
- AUTHORS' COLLECTION

Bench screw.

Wooden fids for splicing rope, rope being in itself an essential farm tool.

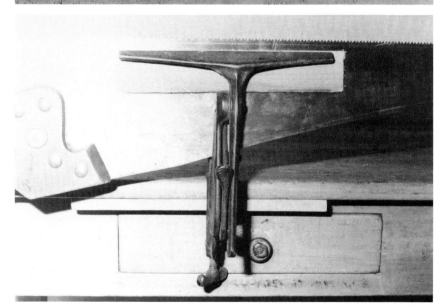

Saw vice.

The *Canada Farmer*, elsewhere in the same issue, advises immigrants to buy more than one good axe and a good grindstone and to treat them with care.

The principal tools that were used for the major construction or maintenance tasks have already been described in relationship to farm activities, but many other tools were generally useful, and could and did end up in the woodworking shop of the farm.

Adzes

For practical application these existed in three forms, and found popular acceptance in the Valley — the heavy polled carpenter's adze for smoothing and driving, the shipwright's adze with its spur for countersinking spikes and the gutter adze for hollowing.

Augers

The two-handed screw augers, bits for the boring machine, tap augers used for enlarging holes, and nose augers were characteristic of the boring tools used.

Axes

In addition to the working axes already discussed, the broad axe, the felling axe and the hewing and shingling hatchet, there was a lathing hatchet available for nailing and cutting plastering lath. Its shape allowed its use right to the ceiling. There was, too, an oddly shaped claw hatchet which served as an axe and as a claw hammer.

Awls

The scratch awl preceded the pencil as a marking tool. The scratched lines it produced can still be seen on early dovetailed drawers, where the awl was used to indicate the location of the cut.

The brad awl had a chisel-like point and was designed for making starting holes for such items as hinge screws, and picture frame brads.

Bevel

The bevel belonged to a group of tools that included the carpenter's square, the mitre square and the try square. It operated on the same principle as any set square except that the angle of its blade could be set at any angle up to 90 degrees from its handle. It was used as a guide in marking material at a desired angle.

Bench Screws

The usual type of wood vice was made with a wooden or steel bench screw fitted with wooden jaws. It held material firmly in position for subsequent work upon it.

Bits

Bits were made to fit the receptacle of a brace, and ordinarily were screw bits. However, they could be countersink, screwdriver or spoke trimmer bits, all for use with a brace.

Brace

A brace was a tool to assist in boring or shaping wood, or driving screws. It was in the form of a crank with a freely rotating hub at one end and, at the other, a receptacle for holding boring bits, shaping tools and screw drivers. The operator pushed against the hub as he rotated the crank to obtain the necessary pressure and circular motion.

Clamps

Clamps, made in cast iron, steel and wood, were used to hold wood in place during the glue-setting process, or while being joined or worked upon.

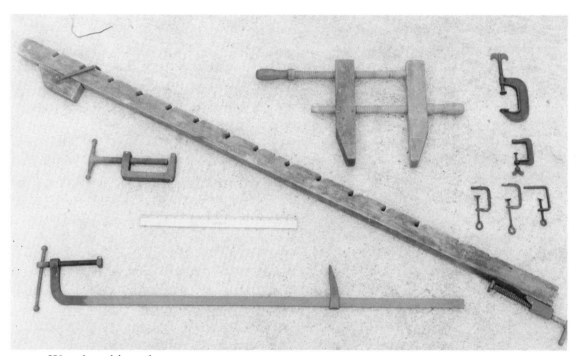

Woodworking clamps. - AUTHORS' COLLECTION

Chisels

The common chisel seen in the carpenter shop is known as a forming chisel. A heavier framing chisel of similar form was used to trim out mortises. The mortising chisel could be used to cut a mortise without pre-drilling. The large slick was used like a plane for smoothing when framing a building. The skew chisel had the cutting edge set at an angle to the chisel blade and was useful for cleaning out mortise corners. The gouge in its many forms was used for hollowing.

Compasses, Dividers and Calipers

Calipers were designed to measure inside and outside diameters, dividers to measure the distance between two points, and compasses to draw a circle of any given radius. These were made in metal and in wood, and applied to measurements for metal or woodworking.

Compass; outside calipers; dividers.
- AUTHORS' COLLECTION

Wooden compass.
- BLOCKHOUSE MUSEUM, MERRICKVILLE

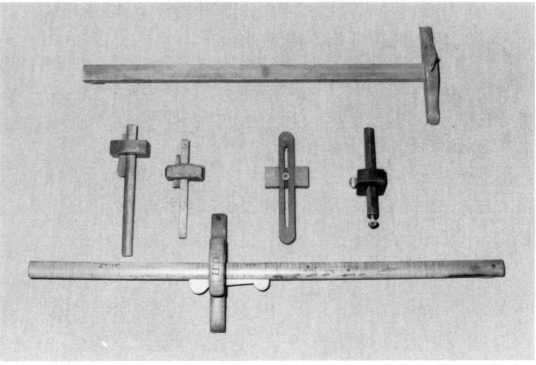

Gauges — note panel gauge at bottom, made from tiger maple.
- AUTHORS' COLLECTION

Drill Stock

This was a geared equivalent of a brace but was normally used for drilling metals with an appropriately tempered drill.

Files

Files existed for the reduction of wood and metal surfaces in the processes of shaping, smoothing and sharpening. They appeared in many shapes to adapt to the contours of the object worked on.

Gauges

Gauges were used to make a line on wood to mark the depth or distance to which a board should be cut, split or planed. A gauge consisted of a block sliding on a rod which had a scribing pin near one end. When secured at the right measurement by either a wedge or set screw, the block was slid along an edge of the board, and the pin inscribed the appropriate parallel mark.

Planes

Three basic planes were common — a short smoothing plane, a general-purpose jack plane and a longer trying plane, particularly useful for long surfaces to be glued. Plow planes (in pairs) for cutting tongue and groove joints and rabbet planes for cutting a "step" on the edge of a board to be fitted to a step on another, again were used in joining. Carpenters had dozens of specialized moulding planes for making door, window and baseboard mouldings, but these were specialist's tools.

Frame saw.
- AUTHORS' COLLECTION

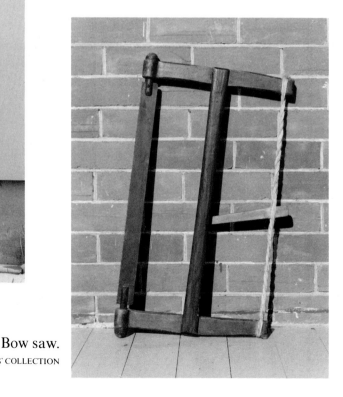

Bow saw.
- AUTHORS' COLLECTION

Plumb Bob

This was simply a weight to be suspended on a string against which the builder could test his uprights for true vertical line.

Saws

The frame saw and the bow saw both had narrow flexible blades and were constructed with wooden frames and tightening devices to provide the blade with the rigidity necessary for effective sawing. The open saw, such as the handsaw and the lumberman's large cross-cut saw, were heavy enough to maintain their own rigidity. Hand-saws were divided into cross-cut saws with bevelled cutting teeth for sawing across the grain, and rip saws with chisel-like teeth for sawing along the grain. Back saws, of which the mortise saw is one, had thin blades for fine work and had to be reinforced with a bar along the top. Keyhole or compass saws, with their narrow tapering blades, were used for cutting shapes such as privy seat holes.

In addition to all the woodworking tools, there were interesting associated items such as glue pots, paint brushes, graining brushes, combs and rollers, and stencils for the borders of painted walls. The contemplation of how some of these were used offers some real challenges to the imagination.

Effective maintenance of tools always has been a problem, but dull or loose or broken tools cannot accomplish an effective job. The farmer's work tools included saw vices and files, oil stones to keep chisel and plane blades sharp, and grindstones and scythe stones to maintain a keen edge on axes, sickles and the blades of grain cradles.

Assorted paint brushes. - AUTHORS' COLLECTION

Water-heated glue pot.
- AUTHORS' COLLECTION

Cobbler's tools — clockwise l. to r.: cobbler's hammer; end-cutting nippers; peg break; curved awl; leather-slicing knife; hand vise; top and bottom — assorted shoe lasts. - AUTHORS' COLLECTION

Harness-makers vice.
- AUTHORS' COLLECTION

Primitive harness vices.
- AUTHORS' COLLECTION

SHOE AND HARNESS REPAIR

By the 1860s factory-made shoes were available. Nevertheless many villages had resident shoemakers and itinerant ones sought trade among the scattered farms. However, then and for decades thereafter, the repair of shoes was usually the responsibility of the farmer.

Few century farm sales fail to produce at least some of the commoner tools of the cobbler's art. The cobbler's hammer is a characteristic shape, as are the upper and sole leather knives and the sewing and pegging awls. Little packages of leatherworker's needles turn up in unexpected places, such as sewing machine drawers. Also to be found are balls of linen thread and chunks of beeswax to waterproof and strengthen the thread. Occasionally a jar or tin partly full of wooden shoe-pegs will be uncovered.

Twice in the authors' collecting career we have come upon whole boxes of hand-formed shoe lasts at farm sales. It seems possible that they represent the foot size of the father and mother and the growth of family feet from the toddler to the adult. It is difficult to determine whether they were associated with a truly gifted head of the household who could make shoes for his family, or if they were made and used by an itinerant shoemaker or his village equivalent, and stored with the family between visits. It appears quite certain that at least some farmers were skilled enough to make moccasins for members of their families.

In the dust at the bottom of old home cobbler's tool boxes can be found dusty paper sole patterns, headless tapered nails in rectangular section, known as sprigs, and long coarse pig bristles. Much of the material found is self-explanatory, but the idea of sewing with a pig bristle attached to a linen thread is novel to us today, as is also the thought of attaching soles to uppers by means of wooden pegs driven with a cobblers hammer through holes already made with pegging awls. There was even a special file, known as a peg break, to smooth off the pegs after they were driven into the shoe. Pegs were substituted for thread for attaching soles to uppers because the constant moisture to which shoes were subjected caused rapid deterioration of the thread.

Shoemaking or repair was only part of the leatherworking responsibility of the farmer. The harness maker's vise was found in simple or more sophisticated form throughout the farming community. Similar awls, needles and waxed thread, plus rings and hooks, snaps, rivetting hammers and rivets, leather cutters and punches maintained the leather harnesses, hobbles, halters and belts, and all the necessary leather and canvas equipment. A broken harness trace was as significant in horsepower days as is a broken driveshaft on a car or truck today. The great difference is that today money is usually more plentiful than time, whereas the reverse was the case in the Confederation decades.

Maple sap collecting
equipment — top to
bottom: wooden spiles;
brace and bit; tin and
wooden sap buckets;
cast iron spile with
copper wire to lead sap
to trough.
- AUTHORS' COLLECTION

Wooden sap bucket.
- AUTHOR'S SKETCH

Cauldron or "cooler". - AUTHORS' COLLECTION

CHAPTER 4
HARVESTING NATURE

POTASH

Canadian potash was in great demand for the making of soap and glass, for use in the textile industry and for the production of explosives. In fact, for much of the nineteenth century, potash was one of Canada's most important exports. It was derived principally from hardwood ashes which the settler had in abundance as he cleared his land of its forest cover.

The farmer probably did not benefit in this way from his first hasty clearing efforts as, for potash production, the hardwood ashes had to be gathered before their salts had been leached away by rain. He had, therefore, to provide a clean, weatherproof ash house in which to keep the ashes until they were disposed of. The ashes could be sold in their raw form to potasheries which were scattered through the countryside, or he could obtain a premium price by processing them and producing potash to sell to the potasheries for final refining.

To produce potash the farmer had first to have a leach. For the production of potash in large quantities leaches were usually hopper-shaped containers made in two thicknesses of heavy boards, as compared to the smaller barrel leaches used in connection with home production of soap.

After putting a layer of straw in the bottom to act as a sieve, the farmer filled the leach nearly to the top with wood ash which he packed down firmly. Water was then poured into the top of the leach, to reappear some hours or days later at the bottom, laden with the alkaline potassium carbonate. This solution was known as the ley.

The ley was then boiled at a high heat in specially-manufactured potash kettles, until, with many of its impurities burned away, it became a molten salt. This was then poured into smaller cauldrons called "coolers," where it solidified as a greyish-green crystalline substance known as potash. The potasheries which purchased this product reheated it to very high temperatures to produce a glistening white substance known as pearl ash, which was sold to industries such as glass and soap producers.

Fortunately for the farmer, the potash trade remained buoyant throughout the period of clearing and surplus timber. Eventually the discovery of mineral deposits provided a cheaper source of potassium products, and the production of potash from organic sources became a thing of the past.

MAPLE SUGAR MAKING

The native peoples of North America were tapping the maple for their only source of sweetening before the white man came. When Philemon Wright and his group of settlers arrived at the Chaudière in March, 1800, the natives were in the

Hand-sled for gathering
maple sap —
approximately 100 cm
(40 in.) long.
- LYALL CLARKE COLLECTION

Snowshoes were often
required for mobility in
sugaring operations.
- AUTHORS' COLLECTION

Birch bark Indian
mokuks for food storage
including maple sugar.
- AUTHORS' COLLECTION

middle of their sugar-making activities. The white settlers were able to improve the methods considerably because they possessed superior tools and implements, and by the mid-nineteenth century, most farm families who had maple trees on their land were producing enough sugar to satisfy their own needs and provide a cash-producing harvest. Some were using the most up-to-date sugar-making equipment available, and others simple and primitive methods.

In all probability by this time most farmers had thinned out their maple woods so that a team and sled could pass comfortably through to collect the sap. To "bleed" or tap the tree, some notched the trunk in a "V" with an axe, drove in a gouge-shaped tapping iron at the base of the notch, and inserted a long slice of pine, cedar or tin with a groove down the centre to guide the sap flowing from the tree to the receptacle. Some bored a hole with a brace and bit, and inserted a spile or spigot made of a long piece of drilled pine or cedar. The sap was caught in troughs hewn out of 75 to 90 centimetre (2½ to 3 feet) lengths of poplar or basswood logs, split in half and hollowed with an axe or an adze. Wooden or tin sap buckets were also used at this time. Tin was the cleanest and best. Wooden sap buckets were made in the truncated cone style (diagram) to keep the hoops from falling off in use or storage. Tin buckets were shaped in reverse to enable them to be nested when put away at the end of the sugaring season.

For each litre of maple syrup produced, the farmer had to boil away some 35 to 40 litres of water from the sap. This took time, quantities of dry and seasoned firewood, and large receptacles in which to reduce the sap. The same cauldrons were probably used for scalding hogs, making soap and cooling the molten potash. This explains the term "cooler" often used in the Valley to describe the cauldron used to boil the sap, an apparent contradiction in terms. Flat evaporator pans made of sheet iron were a great improvement. They were placed over the fire on a framework known traditionally as an arch. The process could be even further refined by installing the evaporator pans at different levels, so that there was a steady flow established from the sap storage vat to the first evaporator pan, and from the other end of this pan by a siphon into the finishing pan. Here the sap was boiled until the product, when cooled, became syrup or sugar, depending on the degree of concentration of the hot syrup.

During the boiling process the sap was cleansed by constantly skimming off the residue which floated to the surface. Skimmers varied in size and appearance, but not in purpose. If sugar was to be produced the hot syrup was poured into wooden or iron moulds to produce substantial blocks or fanciful shapes, depending on the purpose of the producer.

Some sugar operations ran night and day, with the boiling being done in the open and the workers protected from the elements by a lean-to or shed. Other farmers provided more elaborate accommodation, having built the characteristic sugar shack with its large ventilator on top to let the steam escape, and the lean-to attached to provide dry wood storage. These farmers could limit operations to the daylight hours, thus maintaining better product control.

The maple sugar makers of Quebec are famous for the fanciful carved wooden moulds in traditional motifs which they designed. Many have found their way into museums or private collections. There were single and two-piece moulds in geometric, animal and bird designs, and multiple-piece moulds that produced log cabins, hearts or even Bibles.

Maple sugar molds — Quebec. - DIANE SIMARD COLLECTION

Maple sugar cutter — Quebec. - DIANE SIMARD COLLECTION

As in so many other Valley farm activities, the production of maple sugar was a family enterprise. The men traditionally chopped and stored the wood to dry and did most of the collection of the sap, but the women and children helped in the boiling or wherever they were needed. All shared in the neighbourhood parties which so often took place as the boiling came to an end. They were a celebration of a harvest, and also of the end of a long Valley winter.

THE LUMBER CAMPS

Lumbering in the Ottawa Valley was founded on the vast primeval forest of white pine growing on the dry sand and plains that once formed the floor of the long-vanished Lake Algonquin. Here also grew hardwood forests with oak, ash, sugar maple, butternut, walnut and birch. While these were marketable timber, it was the lofty white pine which gave the Valley its first claim to international attention.

In the first half of the nineteenth century most of the timber being exported was rafted down the Ottawa and the St. Lawrence to Quebec to be loaded onto ships bound for England. The logs were squared and formed into small individual rafts called cribs, which, in turn, were assembled into larger rafts. This was done so that the great rafts could be dismantled for running the timber slides, and then reassembled at the bottom for the trip to Quebec. By the 1870s, however, the demand for squared timber for export to Europe was rivalled by the need for sawn lumber in the United States, resulting in a substantial growth in the sawmilling industry throughout the Valley.

The shanty farmer played a unique role in the development of logging in the Ottawa Valley, as well as contributing to economic growth through the sale of his surplus agricultural products to the lumber camps. Both logging and farming are seasonal, in that they have long periods of manpower-intensive activity, interspersed with stretches of relative inactivity. Thus, after harvest, the farmer could sign on with a lumber company, sometimes taking with him the team of farm horses, and become part of a lumber shanty crew, returning to his farm just before spring break-up. It was a hard life. Six days a week he was awakened in time to have his breakfast and get to the cutting site by dawn, and he returned to the shanty after evening had closed down operations. If he were a teamster, he arose an hour earlier to feed his animals. In return he received good food and lodging for his team and himself, and pay in cash for the number of days worked. He returned home with money to help meet family and operating expenses, and in time for the spring work on the farm.

While in the bush the lumber crew had one purpose — to produce the maximum possible number of marketable logs from the timber limit of the company for whom they worked. This crew included axemen, sawyers, teamsters, cooks, clerks and maintenance men, depending upon the size of the shanty. Not only had timber to be cut, but roadways made, slipways prepared, hills cleared of snow on the steep grades of roads and sanded to prevent "runaways." Supplies had to be transported and tallied, and production accurately recorded. It was a complex operation, culminating in the delivery to the frozen tributary streams of the larger rivers of sticks of timber that had been cut by fellers with felling axes, topped and

The lumber shanty. - ONTARIO ARCHIVES REF. ACC. 9118-92

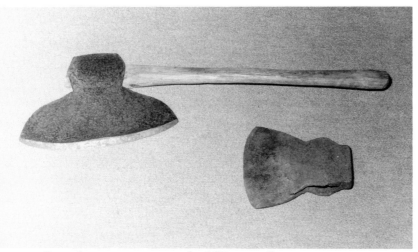

Broad axes — one marked "Bytown".
- AUTHORS' COLLECTION

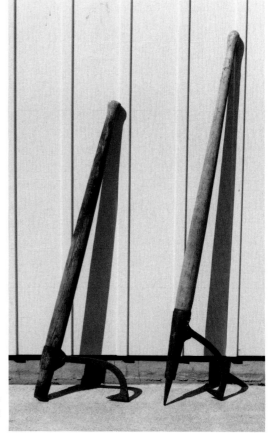

Cant hook and peavey.
- AUTHORS' COLLECTION

Lumber rafts, Barrack Hill, Ottawa. - ONTARIO ARCHIVES REF: L 264

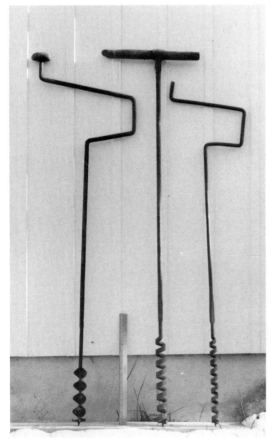

Pick hammers. - AUTHORS' COLLECTION

Raft augers. - AUTHORS' COLLECTION

debranched by logmakers, marked by scorers with scoring axes and trimmed to a square dimension by a skilled hewer with a broad axe.

The broad axe was basically a 5 to 7 kilogram (12 to 15 pound) swung chisel, that literally planed a log smooth. With its offset handle, it reached its zenith of effectiveness in use in the North American woods, mainly because of market demand and the skills developed by the hewers — the cream of the axemen.

Shanty lumbering was sometimes carried out by farmer jobbers, who contracted to harvest the timber crop from an area sublet to them by a large timber company. The logs they cut were sold to the company, and their life had the challenge of the entrepreneur, rather than simply that of a woodsworker. Braddish Billings was an early jobber for Philemon Wright. The jobber's camps were smaller, but similar in style and methods to those of the big shanties, and they used the same equipment in the woods. Their employees were usually relatives and neighbouring farmers.

The felling axes, scoring axes and broad axes were usually made by local industries in centres such as Hull, Renfrew, Pembroke and Ottawa. The imported crosscut saws were first used only for cutting a fallen tree into logs, but later were employed to fell trees as well. Logs were rolled into position using cant hooks, and were held on the sleds for transportation with heavy logging chains. The logs were sledded to the slipways. Problems arose around this mode of transportation. One of these was that snow and ice tended to cake in the frog of the horses' hooves. To break this out each sled carried a special pick-hammer, which normally hung from the harness, and which had to be used from time to time on the trail.

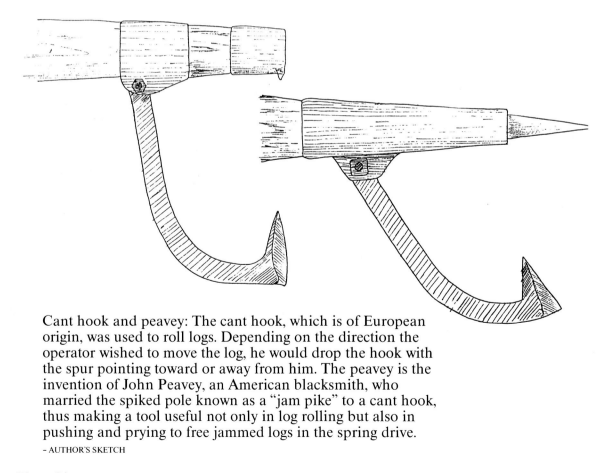

Cant hook and peavey: The cant hook, which is of European origin, was used to roll logs. Depending on the direction the operator wished to move the log, he would drop the hook with the spur pointing toward or away from him. The peavey is the invention of John Peavey, an American blacksmith, who married the spiked pole known as a "jam pike" to a cant hook, thus making a tool useful not only in log rolling but also in pushing and prying to free jammed logs in the spring drive.

– AUTHOR'S SKETCH

When spring came, the woodsmen were paid off and the farmers returned to their farm labours. Left behind to close the camps and prepare for the spring log drive were the rivermen, with their pike poles, peaveys and cant hooks, who stayed to move the logs down to the Ottawa to be made into cribs and rafts.

The process of crib and raft-making required the use of characteristic tools. Logs were moved about using 3 to 5 metre (10 to 15 foot) long pike poles to pull or push the logs into position. Raft shackles formed of two forged spikes and an interconnecting short length of chain served to hold the logs in position. The cribs and rafts were held together with hardwood saplings used as pins, driven into auger holes made with a raftsman's auger, which was used in a standing position. It was about 1.5 metres (5 feet) long, had a crank like a brace at the top end, and an auger bit welded to the bottom end.

If one were to add to the collection of axes, saws, pikes, peavies, cant hooks and augers, such accessories as files, saw sets and a grindstone for sharpening axes, one would have listed the basic hand tools that the shanty-men used in extracting and transporting the tremendous wealth of timber that came out of the woods of the Ottawa Valley.

THE WOODLOT

Firewood

Before the eventual introduction of coal, wood was the only common household and industrial fuel throughout the Valley. It was not an easy commodity to maintain in continuous supply, despite the fact that the area was literally hewn from the woods. In fact this clearing had been so sweeping in its effects that the farmer, by the middle of the nineteenth century, had sometimes to go afield to satisfy the need for firewood on his farm.

The supplying of this fuel began with the felling of a tree, which was then cut into logs by the use of a crosscut saw or an axe, depending on the size of the tree. This was usually done in the autumn after the leaves had fallen, and the trees were dormant. When the snow was deep enough, the logs were skidded out to sleds and brought to the farmyard or woodyard, where they were sawn to cordwood or stovewood length, using a single or two-man crosscut saw, or the familiar bucksaw, a descendant of the frame saw of earlier times.

The stovewood size billets had then to be split with an axe or with a sledge and splitting wedge, and stacked, preferably in a woodshed or other protected storage, to dry for a year before being used.

The hardwoods, such as maple, birch, ash and oak, were considered the most desirable for fuel. They produced a clean, long-burning fire with maximum heat output for the size of the wood. In an open fire they did not explode into sparks as did cedar, and unlike pine and spruce, they produced less resinous smoke to contribute to the problem of dangerous stove-pipe and chimney soot build-up.

Farmers along the rivers had a source of income from selling firewood to passing steamboats. Cut into cordwood lengths, it was stacked at the waterside where it was in considerable demand during the steamboating era on the Ottawa and the Rideau.

Buck saws. - AUTHORS' COLLECTION

Saw buck. - OTTAWA VALLEY FARM

Sledges.
- AUTHORS' COLLECTION

Lumber

Prime trees in the woodlot were set aside to be used when the farmer needed a supply of lumber. He would cut what he required, transport it to the sawmill, and have it custom sawn on a share basis. If he had prime timber and no immediate use for it himself, it was usually in demand for local construction purposes, and could be sold as logs or lumber.

Ice

From the beginning of settlement the farm wife found it necessary to make butter and sometimes cheese for family use. Any surplus was sold or bartered. There was no large production of dairy products for marketing until after the 1850s. There were exceptions like Braddish Billings who, by 1851, was producing large amounts of cheese from a sizable herd of cows. However, as the farmer turned from wheat to mixed farming, commercial dairying developed. Sometimes this was on the basis of one farmer with a limited number of cows setting up a butter or cheese making operation, or a group of farmers supplying milk to a creamery or cheese factory.

To make dairying successful it was necessary to be able to provide cleanliness for the milk supply, pre-cooling of milk, and prompt action in the use of the milk. The cooling requirements of the dairy operations expanded the harvesting and storage of ice, as milk was cooled by such devices as floating a tin bucket containing ice in the vat of milk, and agitating the milk. Another practice was to place the warm milk in 45 litre (10 gallon) milk cans, and then put the can in cold water. This was much more effective if blocks of ice were dumped into the cooling trough. To meet the cooling requirements a supply of ice, sufficient to cover warm weather operation at least, was harvested from convenient lakes and rivers or ponded streams.

Ice kept best when harvested in the coldest weather. The harvesting crew, probably a group of neighbouring farmers, arrived by sled with their ice-cutting tools. The object was to cut a neat array of blocks of consistent size for effective storage.

A hole was first cut, using an axe and an ice chisel, to enable an ice saw to be inserted. Ice sawing was a cold and laborious business, and the sawyer dared not stop cutting while the saw still remained in the ice, lest it freeze immovably into the ice sheet. The saw enabled the harvesters to fashion the blocks squarely, for the better the fit of the ice in the ice house, the better it kept, and the easier it was to load for hauling.

Once the block had been cut free from the surrounding ice, it would be recovered from the water using ice tongs. Sometimes horses were used to pull the block out, sometimes men did it manually. Sometimes a derrick made of four poles with a balancing pole suspended from them, somewhat like a well sweep, was employed to lift the ice blocks out and swing them over to the waiting sled.

Ice tongs, usually blacksmith-forged, varied widely in size, depending on their use. The large tongs used to remove the blocks from the water were cumbersome and unnecessary when handling the ice in the ice house, or in carrying smaller chunks into the milk house.

The ice house was usually a separate double-walled building, with good drainage, good ventilation and as much protection as possible from the sun. While ice could be packed with a substantial layer of straw, chaff or tan bark as an insulator, the best packing material by far was sawdust. The insulating power of sawdust was so effective that a well-packed ice harvest, put in place in cold weather and properly packed with sawdust in a good building, could last for several years.

Ice chests, the predecessor of today's refrigerator, were available at this time, but were probably more common in urban areas. At least one model was grand enough to be advertised as suitable for the dining room.

The ice house was a place for the winter storage of frozen pork, venison or beef, in carcass or in barrels. Such stored barrels, packed in straw ,or sawdust, stayed fully frozen during periods of winter thaw.

Associated with the use of ice were numerous small tools such as ice hatchets, ice mallets (with an ice pick head) and ice picks. All of these were used for cutting large chunks into smaller ones in the ice house, or chipping ice into pieces to crush for the making of ice cream or for any other purpose.

Ice cutting on the Ottawa. - PUBLIC ARCHIVES OF CANADA REF. PR 8932

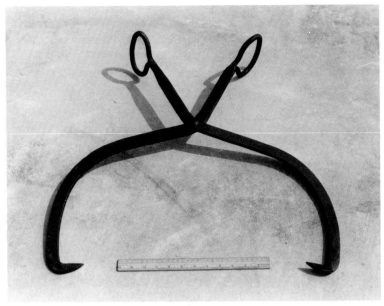

Ice tongs. - AUTHORS' COLLECTION

Ice saw.
- BLOCKHOUSE MUSEUM,
MERRICKVILLE

Ice chest — also termed refrigerator.
- PRIVATE COLLECTION

Game

In the early days of settlement in the Ottawa Valley, fish and game were readily available. Few but the native peoples had been fishing and hunting in the area, and the rivers ran clear and unpolluted. Naturally the newcomers built their mills on the river banks to harness the power and pollutants freely entered the waters, sawdust being one of the most frequent. The cutting down of so much of the forest and the amount of game taken soon began to deplete the seemingly unlimited supplies. However, the remaining resources of fish, waterfowl, upland birds, deer, rabbits and racoons provided sport and pot hunting, and brought some variety to the farm table.

The muzzle loader with percussion caps and the breech loading rifle and shotgun made shooting a simpler and more effective means of obtaining game than did the older flintlock guns. White-tailed deer, moose and bear were hunted not only for food but also for their skins.

Deer skins were scraped and nailed to the sides of buildings to dry for later use. They were then used as rawhide strips or were tanned. Moosehide was the most durable of the skins, but the settlers also made good use of the excellent leather from bear pelts. Fox, wolves, racoons, beaver and muskrat were used also for food by woodsmen.

Deadfalls were constructed for trapping and snare wire and spring traps were also used. An 1865 hardware catalogue includes four full two column pages of such items as powder flasks, shot pouches, percussion caps and melting ladles for making shot. It lists spring traps suitable for mink, fox, otter, beaver, wolf and bear. In the case of one large bear trap, with a jaw spread of 40 centimetres (16 inches), the advertising claimed that it was strong enough to hold a grizzly bear or a moose. Several patterns were available, and local blacksmiths added their skills and imagination by developing custom traps with steel teeth welded to the jaws, and other so-called "improvements".

Animal trap — blacksmith-made spring type.
- AUTHORS' COLLECTION

Powder flask and melting ladle.
- AUTHORS' COLLECTION

The beaver pelts were opened flat and dried on a withe frame, but muskrat, mink, otter and similar skins were taken off the animals in the round, as if rolling off one's socks. They were then stretched and dried, with the fur inside, on oblong board forms of dimensions suited to the size of the animal.

By the 1860s Valley residents could still catch trout, whitefish, bass, pickerel, pike, maskinonge (muskies), sturgeon and eels, although in diminishing quantities. Many were taken on rod and line, but much fishing was done by spear, by gill or dip netting or by the use of traps. Spear fishing, usually with blacksmith-made fish spears, was often done at night with the use of a cresset or "jack light" full of burning pine knots to attract the fish to boat or shore. Winter brought ice fishing, then as now.

Turtles and frogs were objects of the pot hunter, and were part of the rich supply of wildlife that is still characteristic of marshy areas of the Valley today.

Personal narratives of lumber shanty life tell how the monotony of shanty food also was relieved by the hunting and fishing forays of the shanty men on their only free day, Sunday.

Guns are a special study unto themselves. Their use, care and maintenance involved a multitude of accessory items including powder flasks, shot pouches, melting ladles, bullet moulds, percussion caps, gun wads, wad cutters and gun cleaning implements.

Fishermen were well catered to by the manufacture of fish hooks in great variety, including some on silk or gut leaders, artificial flies, silk, cotton or linen fishlines, gill nets, dip nets and fishing creels. For many rural families, however, fishing equipment consisted of a pole cut from the woods, fitted with a simple line and hook, and baited with anything from crayfish to bacon rind.

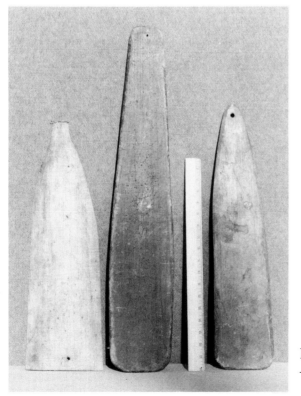

Fish spears.
- AUTHORS' COLLECTION

Pelt stretchers.
- AUTHORS' COLLECTION

CONCLUSION

WHEN you have finished reading this story, and before you put the book aside and return to the twentieth century, perhaps some among you will be moved to plan a trip to Ottawa and a sentimental drive through the National Capital Region, taking in both sides of the Ottawa River. It is a fascinating area, and, after all, it belongs to all Canadians.

The Valley landscape is still dotted with majestic early barns, some crumbling into ruins, others maintained and still in use. The log house survives in the same varied state, except that its smaller size has encouraged those who admire its structure and proportions to dismantle some and move them to new sites in order to preserve them. We now find them being used in several ways, such as tourist information centres, small museums or in reconstructed villages. There are even log building collectors who move them to their own properties to save them for future generations to enjoy. Some of the Confederation era farm and village homes are still in the possession of the original families, while others are being renovated and occupied by those who have discovered their gracious proportions and fine craftsmanship.

Collecting log buildings is not for everyone but it is still possible to own one or two of the tools used by the builders, or at least to see those tools in museums or in actual use at pioneer villages. We handle these surviving artifacts with a healthy respect and paraphrase Ralph Waldo Emerson in saying "They builded better than they knew."

Job completed —
photographer's
assistant.

BIBLIOGRAPHY

A "Canuck". *Pen Pictures of Early Pioneer Life in Upper Canada*. William Briggs, Toronto, 1905. Coles Publishing Company Facsimile edition, Toronto, 1974.

Abrahamson, Una. *Crafts Canada — The Useful Arts*. Clarke Irwin, Toronto, 1974.

Armstrong, Audrey I. *Harness in the Parlour — A Book of Early Canadian Facts and Folklore*. Musson Book Company, Toronto, 1974.

Arthur, Eric and Witney, Dudley. *The Barn — A Vanishing Landmark in North America*. McClelland and Stewart, Toronto, 1972.

Bedore, Bernie. *The Shanty — Part I of The Big Pine*. Mufferaw Enterprises, Arnprior, Ontario, 1963.

Bélisle, Louis-Alexandre. *Les outils manuels*. Bélisle, Éditeur, Inc., Québec, 1969.

Blake, Verschoyle Benson and Greenhill, Ralph. *Rural Ontario*. University of Toronto Press, 1969.

Bond, Courtney C.J. *The Ottawa Country — A Historical Guide to the National Capital Region*. The Queen's Printer, Ottawa, 1968.

Brault, Lucien. *Ottawa Old & New*. Ottawa Historical Information Institute, Ottawa, 1946.

Breckenridge, Muriel. *The Old Ontario Cookbook*. McGraw-Hill Ryerson, Toronto, 1976.

Brett, K.B. *Women's Costume in Early Ontario*. Royal Ontario Museum Series, the Governors of the University of Toronto, 1966.

Brown, Howard Morton. *Founded Upon a Rock — Carleton Place Recollections*, 150th Year Festival Committee 1969-1970, Carleton Place, Ontario, 1969.

Boyd, J.A. *Summary of Canadian History From the Time of Cartier's Discovery to the Present Day*. James Campbell and Sons, Toronto, 1874.

Carr-Harris, Bertha Wright. *The White Chief of the Ottawa*. William Briggs, Toronto, 1903.

Craig, Sara B. *Hello Nepean*. Merivale Pioneer Historians, Ottawa, 1974.

Davies, Blodwen. *Ottawa, Portrait of a Capital*. McGraw-Hill, Toronto, 1954.

Dickie, Donalda. *The Great Adventure — An Illustrated History of Canada for Young Canadians*. J.M. Dent & Sons, Toronto, 1951.

Dubé, Françoise and Genest, Bernard. *Arthur Tremblay — Forgeron de village*. Bibliothèque nationale du Québec, Québec, 1978.

Dupont, Jean-Clause. *L'artisan forgeron*. Les Presses de l'Université Laval, Québec, 1979.

Dupont, Jean-Claude. *Le sucre du pays*. Leméac, Montréal, 1975.

Eggleston, Wilfred. *The Queen's Choice*. National Printing Bureau, Ottawa, 1961.

Evans, Patrick, M.O. *The Wrights*. National Capital Commission, Ottawa, 1967.

Finnigan, Joan. *Some of the stories I told you were true*. Deneau Publishers, Ottawa, 1981.

Fowke, Edith. *Folklore of Canada*. McClelland and Stewart, Toronto, 1976.

Genêt, Nicole et Vermette, Lucie et Decardie-Audet, Louise. *Les objets familiers de nos ancêtres*. Les Éditions de l'homme, Montréal, 1974.

Grant, George Monro (ed.). *Picturesque Canada — The Country as It Was and Is*. Vol. III. Belden Brothers, Toronto, 1882.

Greening, W.E. *The Ottawa*. McClelland and Stewart, Toronto, 1961.

Guillet, Edwin C. *Pioneer Settlements in Upper Canada*. University of Toronto Press, 1933.

Hart, Patricia W. *Pioneering in North York — A History of the Borough*. General Publishing Company, Don Mills, 1971.

Historical Atlas of Carleton County. H. Beldon, Toronto, 1879, Facsimile editions, Cummings, Ross (ed.) Port Elgin, 1971.

Historical Society of the Gatineau. *Up the Gatineau!* Old Chelsea, Québec, 1977.

Jeffries, C.W. *The Picture Gallery of Canadian History*, Volumes I, II and III. Ryerson Press, Toronto, 1945.

Jones, Mary Fallis. *The Confederation Generation*. Royal Ontario Museum, Toronto, 1978.

Ladell, John and Ladell, Monica. *Inheritance, Ontario's Century Farms Past & Present*. Macmillan, Toronto, 1979.

Lambert, Richard S. *Renewing Nature's Wealth — A Centennial History of the Public Management of Lands, Forests and Wildlife in Ontario, 1763-1967*. Ontario Department of Lands and Forests, Toronto, 1967.

Legget, Tobert. *Ottawa Waterway — Gateway to a Continent*. University of Toronto Press, Toronto, 1975.

Legget, Robert, *Rideau Waterway*. University of Toronto Press, 1955.

Lessard, Michel and Marquis, Huguette. *Encyclopédie des Antiquités du Québec*. Les éditions de l'homme, Montréal, 1971.

Lett, W.P. *Recollections of Old Bytown*. Bytown Series 3, Bytown Museum, Ottawa, 1979.

MacKechnie, S. Wyman. *What Men They Were!* Pontiac Printshop, Shawville, Québec, 1975.

Massey, Ellen Gray (ed.). *Bittersweet Country*. Anchor Press/Doubleday, New York, 1978.

McGiffen, Verna Ross. *Pakenham — Ottawa Valley Village, 1823-1860*. Mississippi Publishers, Pakenham, Ontario, 1963.

McKenzie, Ruth. *Leeds and Grenville: Their First Two Hundred Years*. McClelland and Stewart, Toronto, 1967.

Medsger, Oliver Perry. *Edible Wild Plants — The Complete Authoritative Guide to Identification and Preparation of North American Wild Plants*. Macmillan, New York, 1972.

Mercer, Henry C. *American Carpenters' Tools*. Buckstown Historical Society, Doylestown, Pennsylvania, 1960.

Milnes, Herbert. *Settlers' Traditions*. The Boston Mills Press, Erin, Ontario, 1977.

Minhinnick, Jeanne. *At Home in Upper Canada*. Clarke Irwin, Toronto, 1970.

Morgan, Carl. *Early Woodenware in Canada*. The Boston Mills Press, Erin, Ontario, 1977.

Morse, Eric. *Fur Trade Canoe Routes of Canada/Then and Now*. Queen's Printer, Ottawa, 1969.

Ondaatje, Kim and Mackenzie, Lois. *Old Ontario Houses*. Gage, Toronto, 1977.

Radcliffe, Thomas (ed.). *Authentic Letters from Upper Canada*. Pioneer Books, Macmillan, 1953.

Reaman, G. Elmore. *A History of Agriculture in Ontario*, Volume I. Saunders, Toronto, 1970.

Rempel, John I. *Building With Wood*. University of Toronto Press, 1967.

Renton, Audrey. *Both Sides of the River — 12 Historical Essays to Commemorate the 100th Anniversary of the Osgood Station Post Office*. Kars Women's Institute.

Richmond "150" Sesquicentennial Yesterday and Today 1818-1968. ([Canada]: n.p., n.d.)

Russell, Loris. *Everyday Life in Colonial Canada*. Copp Clark, Toronto, 1973.

Séguin, R.L. *L'équipement de la ferme canadienne aux XVIIe siècles*. Montréal, Ducharme, 1959.

Shortt, Edward (ed.) *Perth Remembered*. Perth Museum, Perth, Ontario, 1967.

Sloane, Eric. *Diary of an Early American Boy*. Ballantyne Book of Canada Ltd., Toronto, 1974.

Sloane, Eric. *A Museum of Early American Tools*. Ballantyne Books of Canada Ltd., Toronto, 1973.

Smith, Jean and Smith, Elizabeth. *Collecting Canada's Past*. Prentice-Hall, Scarborough, 1974.

Spencer, Audrey. *Spinning and Weaving at Upper Canada Village*. McGraw-Hill Ryerson, Toronto, 19864.

Stevens, Gerald. *In a Canadian Attic*. McGraw-Hill Ryerson, Toronto, 1963.

Thuro, Catherine. *Primitives & Folk Art — Our Handmade Heritage*. Collector Books, Paducah, Kentucky, 1979.

Traill, Catherine Parr. *The Backwoods of Canada*. London, 1846. rpt. Toronto: McClelland and Stewart, 1969.

Traill, Catherine Parr. *The Canadian Settlers' Guide*. Toronto, 1855. rpt. Toronto: McClelland and Stewart, 1969.

Tweedsmuir History Committee, Stittsville Women's Institute. *Country Tales*. 1973.

Walker, Harry. *100 Years Ottawa and the Valley*. Articles appearing in the Ottawa *Journal* from January 28 to March 3, 1967.

Walker, Harry J. "Saga of Upper Canada Settlement." *Canadian Geographical Journal*, Volume LXXXII, No. 3, p. 76, March 1971.

Walker, Harry and Walker, Olive. *Carleton Saga*. Carleton County Council, Runge Press, Ottawa, 1968.

Watson, Aldren A. *The Village Blacksmith*. Thos. Y. Crowell & Co., New York, 1968.

Webster, Donald Blake (ed.). *The Book of Canadian Antiques*. McGraw-Hill Ryerson, Toronto, 1974.

Whitton, Charlotte. *A Hundred Years A-Fellin'*. Gillies Brothers Ltd., Braeside, Ontario, 1974.

Woolman, Mary Schenk and McGowan, Ellen Beers. *Textiles — A Handbook for the Student and the Consumer*. Macmillan, New York, 1914.

INDEX

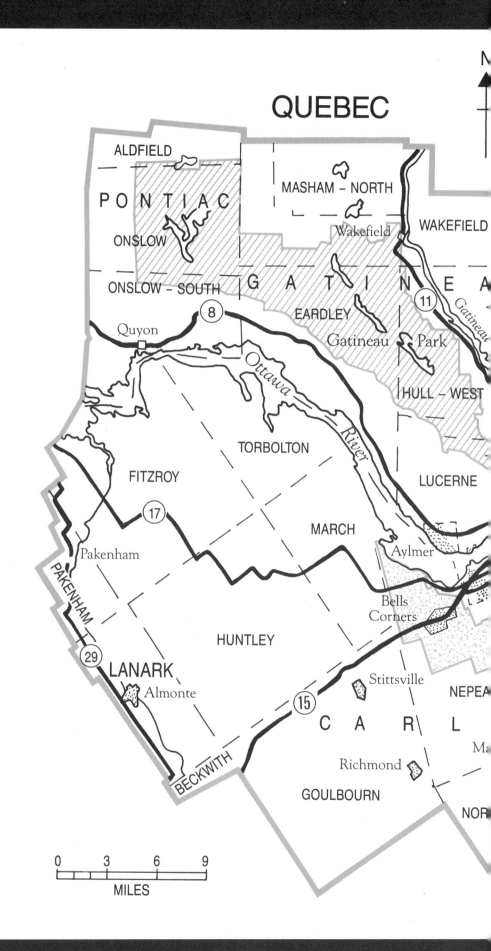